LEGACY OF A
SHOOTING STAR:

Published under licence by Brown Dog Books and
The Self-Publishing Partnership Ltd, 10b Greenway Farm, Bath Rd, Wick, nr.
Bath BS30 5RL, UK

www.selfpublishingpartnership.co.uk

ISBN printed book: 978-1-83952-945-0
ISBN e-book: 978-1-83952-946-7

Cover design by Kevin Rylands
Internal design by Andrew Easton
Illustrations by Andrew Prescott

Printed and bound in the UK

This book is printed on FSC® certified paper

LEGACY OF A SHOOTING STAR:
BEYOND ALCATRAZ

SHAHAB HASHTROUDI

BROWN DOG BOOKS

"May your faith always shine
With Light"

Shab

To Massoud – my beloved brother
Losing you left a hole I couldn't fill,
but writing this helped me carry you forward.
You're in every part of this story.

And to Stavy
You love me, pushed me, believed in me and wouldn't let me quit.
This book only exists because you made sure it did.

For both of you – thank you, always.

CONTENTS

'The name Shahab has Persian origins and translates to meteor or shooting star. This evocative meaning is often associated with brilliance, speed and a fleeting beauty, reflecting the transient beauty of a meteor's journey across the night sky.'

Ancestry.com

PART ONE:
A SHOCK TO THE SYSTEM

CHAPTER ONE: DAWN RAID

The moments before dawn really were the darkest of all on October 21, 2016 when nine strangers barged into my quiet seaside home, changing my life forever. As the antique wall clock struck 5 am at the Dorset property that would be later described in court as a 'luxury residence', the interlopers seized my wallet and car keys and handcuffed me in my underpants. I was not even permitted the privacy of urinating alone in my own bathroom.

It made little difference when the members of this middle-aged gang turned out not to be armed robbers but the enforcement wing of the British taxman, clad in standard-issue navy blue jackets bearing the insignia of Her Majesty's Revenue and Customs. They still ended up stealing my freedom, blemishing a hitherto clean sixty-one-year criminal record, breaking up my marriage and shattering my family.

A few stern strikes of a judge's wooden gavel twenty-five months later, I was incarcerated at Her Majesty's pleasure in Winchester, Dartmoor and Channings Wood prisons for a grey and miserable three years, creating echoes of my family's life without freedom in post-revolutionary Iran. Going straight now, I refuse to let this define me. I am so much more than this part of my life. But, it does have to serve as a preface to my greater story, particularly as I write it now still under licence requiring me to report to probation officers once a month and not stay overnight without permission anywhere other than my home.

The dawn raid has to be one of the biggest shocks I have ever experienced. My wife, Gabriella, a woman of style and elegance, was the only person in the household to be up and about at such as early hour. She was cherishing her habitual daily hour of solitude, a moment of introspection before the beginning of the day's duties at a bustling private school. Our son Sasha was still nestling contentedly in his bed upstairs, the rhythm of his breaths a testament to his tranquil slumber. Thankfully, our daughter, Nicole, was away, busy in the halls of academia. Gaby had just about enough time to brew some coffee, its rich aroma wafting through the air when a sharp rapping at the door shattered her peace without warning. Her eyes darted to the clock; her mind was a whirlwind of confusion as she took steps in trepidation towards our stout wooden front door.

The gang needed only a foot over the threshold and the brandishing of their official credentials and search warrant to gain the entrance they demanded. As Gaby screamed in fear, I was jerked awake, my heart pounding against my ribcage. Clad in Marks & Spencer's finest, I stumbled down the stairs, each step increasing my dread. My nightmares had never been this frightening. Later, I learned that Britain's anti-terrorist legislation had been deployed to facilitate this early morning call. Not for the first time, my Iranian heritage had counted against me.

As I squinted in the sudden artificial light, I was confronted by a lanky thin man, his balding head shining in the luminescence. He thrust his warrant against my chest with a clinical detachment; the words he must have been so accustomed to reading out aloud sounding distant and surreal. Rights that I thought belonged to movie scripts were stripped away; a requested call to my solicitor was denied. As the cuffs made their cold embrace around my wrists for the first of what would become far too many times to recall, I was confronted with what I never got used to: the loss of solitude and an ever-present sense of being constantly watched and monitored – despite there never being any prospect of my attempting to escape.

Rough hands 'assisted' me to dress and dragged my bewildered body back down the stairs, my biceps screaming in protest from their vice-like grip. As an unflinching photographer clicked away, Nicole's GCSE files were being examined and a computer was in the process of being carted out. My unwelcome guests were dissatisfied with the mere £200 in my wallet, scanning my credit cards and demanding my car keys. As they entered my garage, a youthful voice was heard gleefully requesting a more senior investigator for permission to drive my prized Porsche Panamera to the police station.

Marched abruptly into the cold darkness, I was given zero time for goodbyes. Stumbling deliberately to force a pause in the rush so that I could turn awkwardly to meet Gaby's gaze, I immediately wished that I had not done so, her look of unspoken confusion and distress mirroring and magnifying my own. Sasha stood alongside: his shocked and helpless face the last image I saw before being twisted with hobbled wrists into a waiting car reeking of stale vomit and despair. The cuffs were already biting into my wrists. For more than an hour, I sat alone in silence, unseeing as details were slowly etched on the grey silhouettes around me, before a rosy dawn glow fully illuminated the imposing houses in the upmarket Bournemouth cul-de-sac that I had for decades called home. The silence was profane, a yawning void without answers or reassurance. All I could do was revisit the morning's chaos in my mind like a skipping record, each loop bringing fresh bewilderment over the brutal symphony of accusations of fraud, evasion and irregularities made by the men in blue. Back inside my house, the havoc became methodical and thorough. Every drawer was emptied and each cupboard opened; their contents spilled out in an exuberant display of disregard. Gaby's pleas for understanding, for any shred of explanation, were met with silence or dismissive gestures. Somebody had already decided that I was guilty. The home we had built, filled with treasured memories and dreams, was reduced to a mere crime scene.

Unknown to me at that moment, similar scenarios were unfolding at the leafy residences of my brothers Shahin and Hedayat, their sanctuaries breached and defiled by the shadowy tendrils of a wave of coordinated pre-dawn strikes. As I was being whisked on that grey morning to the forbidding edifice of the Poole and Dorset Police Station, a faceless brutalist monolith squatting over the town centre, my disoriented siblings were being cuffed and corralled into the sterile confines of the local constabulary. Paul Podvoiskis, the stalwart director of our restaurants and bars group – ironically, we had named it Alcatraz in complete ignorance of the future incarceration awaiting us – also found his hearth laid siege by the revenue's jackboots.

KAFKAESQUE

Within ninety minutes – the duration of a mere football match – of that initial knock at the door, the four of us were processed through Kafkaesque labyrinths of corridors and holding cells. Fingerprinted, frisked and documented, each sat alone with thoughts, locked in stark interview rooms devoid of any semblance of warmth, with windows replaced by one-way mirrors and daylight surrendered to harsh, buzzing florescent lights. Tables stood bolted to the floor, barriers between captives and interrogators; symbols of the vast gulf already existing between our previous reality and this new surreal nightmare.

Others were dragged into the investigators' orbit. On the stroke of 9 am, the pulsing heart of our business empire on a quiet Bournemouth business park was disrupted, raucous sounds splintering the calm, as a fresh battalion of investigators swarmed Alcatraz's headquarters. As vehicle doors slammed and the staccato tramp of booted footfalls reverberated up stairwells, any lingering vestige of order was rapidly eroded.

The disruption unleashed in those offices above our warehouse mirrored the tumults unfolding across the domestic spheres with uncanny, almost fractal fidelity. As the heavy metal door creaked open, a throng of stern-faced agents flooded the office, their eyes laser-scanning the room. Alison Clark, our petite payroll manager, froze, her heart hammering. As more boisterous members of our team found themselves lost for words, Tracy Shaw, our in-house accountant, breezed into the office unsuspecting, her habitual cheerful smile faltering instantly. Her smile, like the fragile calm of the office, evaporated under the harsh interrogation lights. She too was now a suspect. The relentless questioning began, a brutal marathon that would test Tracy's resilience to its breaking point. Computers were whisked away with all the pomp of criminal evidence, while reams of confidential records were strewn about like frenzied breadcrumbs across each available surface, their contents sifted and dissected with merciless efficiency.

Back in Poole, a duty solicitor eventually arrived and advised me to cooperate fully. It was easy to answer the questions, but hard to satisfy the interrogators who seemed to be in search of an unidentified crime. The barrage of questions, accusations and insinuations twisted my routine business dealings and annual familial visits to Iran into something sinister. Why, I was repeatedly asked, did I visit Iran every year. What cause did I ever have to stop in Dubai on the way? Most menacingly, ISIS, a name carrying the weight of fear and violence, was uttered in the same breath. I reeled in disbelief. Each query about my associations or activities felt like another brick added to an invisible wall that was slowly rising around me, separating me from the life I knew.

The clock's hands seemed to move in slow motion, each tick marking the passage of a reality that grew increasingly distant. Lunchtime came and went, marked only by a stale sandwich and a cup of over-brewed tea I could barely stomach. The officers changed shifts, constantly coming and going, but the questions persisted, circling back time and time again to Iran, Alcatraz's finances operations and that T word – terrorism. With each repetition, my answers remained consistent, my confusion and frustration mounting. The absence of any concrete accusations only added to the surreal nature of the ordeal.

One officer received a call on his smartphone, revealing that someone in the Alcatraz office had spotted a large safe and was asking where the keys were. I directed them to their hiding place and the investigators were delighted with the discovery of what appeared to be a significant pile of cash. They were much less excited when they found that the notes were actually Christmas vouchers, printed 20,000 at a time to give as gifts. I felt relief but no happier when this was clarified. That safe could have contained stolen gold bars, for all the difference it made to our fate at the hands of the clunky, mechanical British judicial system.

I co-operated with questioning, reeling from the revelation that no fewer than forty-five police officers had been involved in the dawn raids. Just think how much more productive they could all have been elsewhere, rather than being drafted to assist the revenue with inquiries we would have been all too happy to satisfy under the usual terms of business conduct. The hours in the cells and the interview room stretched into the evening and the toll of the day's events began to manifest. My initial shock gave way to a weary resignation, the strain of maintaining his composure in the face of such absurdity etching deep lines of fatigue across his brow. The plodding but steely officers showed no sign of relenting, their determination unyielded by the lack of any incriminating evidence.

Finally, as the clock neared 7 pm, marking the end of a day that stretched into an eternity, a sliver of hope pierced my exhaustion. I was free to go but the relief was short-lived, crushed by a stern London-accented voice.

'We'll be bringing you in for questioning again soon.'

The warning hung heavily in the air. Then, as I was cast out of the police station, the cool evening breeze felt like a balm against my skin, a stark contrast to the stifling atmosphere in the interrogation room. The sun, shrouded in clouds, had dimmed. I savoured the moment. Yet, the relief of my release was tempered by the newly formed knowledge that my brothers and colleagues were ensnared in their own battles, their fates also uncertain. The world I stepped back into was not the same as the one I had left behind that morning. The raid, the interrogation, the accusations had irrevocably altered the landscape of my life, setting me on an uncertain path fraught with challenges. Alcatraz had been breached anew, yet its captors wore neither stripes nor shackles.

A RICH COATING OF IRONY

My journey to that chaotic iron staircase felt thick with irony. Sent to school in Salisbury by my wealthy family in pre-revolutionary Iran, I had graduated and, together with my brothers, built up Alcatraz, a chain of eateries around Bournemouth on England's south coast. By September 2008, we had expanded and grown the brand to fifteen sites ranging from independent coffee shops to classy restaurants, glitzy nightclubs and a seventeen-bedroom hotel. We also had a list of country pubs specialising in British food. The livelihoods of more than 350 staff and their families could not have weighed more heavily on my mind.

However, the global financial crisis of 2008 was dramatic and severe. The Royal Bank of Scotland, our main lender, run at that time by Chief Executive Fred 'the Shred' Goodwin, collapsed spectacularly and had to be rescued by the UK government. When the bank, desperate to ensure its own survival, pulled its lending from our companies, we found it impossible in the ensuing liquidity crunch to secure replacement funding. After frantic weeks and months, we were advised that we had no option but to enter voluntary liquidation. Eight years later, it turned out that HMRC was searching for evidence that this liquidation of Alcatraz and ten other companies had been contrived to evade £3.8m of tax.

Despite the speed and urgency of the dawn raid, it took two years for charges to be brought and then another eight weeks for the twelve supposedly true and just jurors to hear our case and deliver their verdict.

But time, as I was to discover, is far from all that is needed for true resolutions to be found in life.

CHAPTER TWO: IN THE DOCK

What is worse: a sudden shock or a prolonged agony? I now know for sure which fate I would opt for. If the dawn raid was unexpected, swift and brutal, my introduction to Britain's legal system involved miscarriages of justice long before I stood in the dock at Southampton Crown Court and pleaded not guilty to charges of accounting fraud. Though the law has yet to acknowledge it, I am still convinced that I and my brothers were deprived of our liberty by a combination of errors, incompetence and prejudice.

The ordeals of the innocent sub-postmasters now accepted to have been prosecuted in error for fraud by the British Post Office endured for many more years than my own case, but I imagine that the residue of feelings left behind is at least slightly similar. My senior barrister left me in the lurch just before my trial, entrusting the task of defending me against highly complex fraud allegations to two junior staffers. During the trial, a near all-white jury was selected. Some jurors fell asleep or played 'hangman'. One was sanctioned for wearing an offensive T-shirt. I feel misconstrued and betrayed, part of a much bigger game in which I was dealt a poor hand and never given much of a chance.

It is still painful to recollect all the details, but, try as hard as I do, I am not able to forget them. A few months after the dawn raid, I was summoned to the police station for further questioning, accompanied by Daniel Berman, a square-jawed, fast-talking senior partner at Renshaw Derrick, a law firm with branches in London and Bournemouth. Berman identified himself as the co-founder, appeared competent and experienced and was quick with ready advice.

'Say "no comment" to all questions.'

Berman wanted to do all the talking, squaring up to the HMRC interrogator.

'You think you can be prosecutor, judge and jury all at the same time,' he kept telling him.

My lead lawyer appeared tough. He was not going to let me be messed about or unfairly accused. He told me he believed in my innocence and was eager to handle my case. His firm of criminal solicitors could get me through this. No mention was made of the much more junior colleagues and lawyers from other firms who would end up representing me. How many cases like mine had they ever handled before? Would they be equipped to represent me as robustly as their leader if he was indisposed for any reason?

After a bleak session of questions from a slack-jawed and robust legal counsel, I was freed from the police station and told that I would be allowed to continue my life and the little that was left of my business. Nearly two years passed and the correspondence with the Crown Prosecution Service and the British taxman was sporadic. At some moments, deeply immersed as I was in attempting to streamline our business operations, it was almost possible to forget the huge weight on my shoulders; the possibilities that were not under my control, the unconscionable threats to my future. But I was never able to forget for long; the reality was that life was suspended. Even without incarceration in a prison cell, I was already living under restriction.

When this period came to an end two years later, it was as abrupt as the original dawn raid. Out of the blue, with no warning, a letter arrived on my doormat from the Crown Prosecution Service, giving notice in stark black ink about a Crown Court trial scheduled for November 18, 2018 at Southampton Crown Court. Charges were laid against me and my brothers, alleging that we had failed to pay VAT and had stolen income tax and national insurance contributions from our employees over eight years. I was to face four charges of cheating the public revenue, while Hedi and Shahin were issued with a single charge.

A GAME OF BLUFF

It was a devastating hammer blow. Berman's bluff had worked on me, at least, leaving me convinced that HMRC lacked sufficient evidence to proceed against me and my brothers. Not for the last time, he turned out to be wrong. Seeking guidance, I approached the straight-as-a-die commercial law firm that had overseen Alcatraz's accounts and business transactions for the past thirty-five years, but to no avail. Criminal law was not its forte, I was told in no short measure, and I was advised to stick with Renshaw Derrick.

I formally engaged Berman, who was to be supported by Tarquin McCalla, a callow-looking barrister who did not exude the same brash confidence as his boss, and Kate Green, an even meeker junior. Other barristers connected to Renshaw Derrick represented my brothers, Paul Podvoiskis and Tracy Shaw.

At least I still had the lawyer who had stood firm with me against my new foe in those HMRC interviews, but not for long. Weeks before my trial was due to begin, Berman stood down from the case, citing an outbreak of tinnitus in his ears that left him unfit to advocate. McCalla, a friend of Daniel's from schooldays, took over but he was unequipped to handle a complex financial fraud case. Kate Green seemed very aptly named, even more out of her depth than her lead barrister. As for Berman, I later discovered that he had ended up leaving Renshaw Derrick to join a new team as an agent in the world of football, attracted no doubt by transfer fees even more lucrative than the £800,000 in legal aid paid to Renshaw Derrick for our trial.

The court case duly started on time and was supposed to last seven weeks. Each morning, we drudged in from Bournemouth to Southampton for a full day on trial. It was a challenging juggling act, considering we still had businesses to run which depended on our attention, especially at the busiest time of the year. Judge Henry, replete in his white wig, presided over the court as I sat with my brothers and the two other defendants in a dock made of glass so thick that we could not follow the proceedings.

'I can't hear a thing,' I told the usher. My complaint was waved away.

Eventually, sets of earphones were found for all the defendants but it was not much of an improvement. I summoned the usher again.

'Excuse me, but I still cannot hear.'

It took an official complaint to the judge before an officer was ordered to unlock the door to the dock so we could hear. That was helpful but the same procedure had to take place every day as new duty officers appeared. Our worried families, mingling with university students and court staff in the public gallery, did not have auditory issues but they still felt lost amid the legal language and complex financial details. Nobody seemed to know what was happening.

Six barristers wearing wigs, half a dozen solicitors, local journalists and HMRC officers filled the busy courtroom. The entire morning of the first day was spent choosing the twelve jurors. Two potential jurors excused themselves, saying they had knowledge of Alcatraz's restaurants, nightclubs, pubs and hotel. Replacements had to be sought but the cast was limited; all the jurors ended up being white Caucasian, except for a tiny elderly Indian lady.

There were four business people, a young woman of about twenty years who was eager to start her university course in Italy, a single mother who unsuccessfully asked to be excused so she could look after her daughter, a teacher and an unemployed man who tried to escape the trial so that he could attend at the job centre. After Judge Henry refused this request, the jobless man ended up securing a new role as foreman of the jury. Our twelve 'fair and free' jurors seemed anything but, appearing almost as unhappy as we were to be in this drab courtroom in the shopping weeks before Christmas. Applications were made to the judge for some time off on Saturdays so they could do their seasonal shopping. The judge was in no mood to agree.

Every morning we sat as the jurors filed to their seats. They seemed to have made up their minds already; I swear I saw hatred on some of those faces.

HANGMAN

During the proceedings, it was noticed that two jurors, a young student and the old Indian woman, were playing the game of hangman as they came and went from the court. One arrived one day at the soulless brutalist courtroom complex wearing a T-shirt bearing a slogan that clearly showed he was not going to give us a chance. Large letters on the front of the shirt proclaimed: 'My naivety is the same as the defendant's stupidity'. The words did not appear to be in keeping with the impartiality he was being asked to observe until the moments of deliberation began.

The youthful Tarquin McCalla leapt to his feet.

'Why is this juror wearing a T-shirt suggesting that he has already made up his mind up on the day that my client is due to begin giving evidence,' he implored.

Judge Henry was firm. 'Ask the juror to provide an explanation,' he told the clerk to the court.

The jurors were sent to their room, accompanied by the court clerk. Half an hour later, she returned and dutifully submitted a written statement from the juror saying that the words on the T-shirt had been intended to apply to all of the defendants.

'Bring the juror before the court,' the judge commanded. The juror appeared, not sheepishly enough for my liking.

'Do the words on your shirt imply that that you have already made up your mind, before hearing from this defendant?' the judge thundered.

'I was only joking,' said the juror, who, only slightly abashed, asked to be allowed to carry on. Every one of the lawyers acting for the five defendants challenged this juror's independence and asked for his removal, but the judge refused, instructing the other members of the jury to not be at all influenced by the matter. The juror arrived for court the next day dressed in a plain white T-shirt. It made no difference. The damage was done.

'A FAMILY LIKE A MAFIA'

During early meetings between all the defence barristers, it had been agreed that none of them would attack or discredit each other or their clients in front of the judge or jury.

However, on several occasions, this pledge was not respected, and happened without being challenged. As Paul Podvoiskis's barrister summed up his client's defence in his closing statement, he described the Hashtroudi family as a 'family like a mafia' that would encourage its workers to commit unlawful acts.

'Imagine a casino in Las Vegas run by the brothers, doing what they want without being questioned,' he told the jury. 'Nobody can challenge them.' McCalla and the other barristers made no challenge, leaving jurors to associate the defendants in our case with what they saw in American legal films and soap operas.

'Why did you not challenge all that stuff about the mafia and Las Vegas?' I asked McCalla during a break in proceedings.

'Trust me on this,' he replied. 'I don't want the jury to dislike me. I want them on my side.' I was still unhappy with what had been said and asked McCalla to intervene. On the last day of the trial, he said he would speak privately to Paul Podvoiskis's barrister, requesting him not to repeat the casino slur. Sadly, it was too late.

On the trial's second day, the prosecutor delved into the calculations of VAT and PAYE in our businesses. Most of the jurors had never run their own business and did not understand technical financial and tax issues. They struggled to comprehend, sending notes to the judge saying that they could not understand. The result was that for the next seven days, attending tax experts from HMRC gave lectures about the workings of the VAT and PAYE systems.

From the glazed looks on the faces of jurors, it did not appear to be helping.

Rising from the uncomfortable wooden chairs in the main body of the courtroom itself, the bald-headed prosecutor was constructing a fantasy so removed from the truth that I barely recognised that his words were supposed to be describing me. He portrayed my personal life, house, children and material possessions as lavish and excessive, my lifestyle as wanton and greedy. The brothers I loved so dearly became in his emotive words hardened criminals.

The ardent prosecutor eulogised about my house, which I had bought with a mortgage forty years previously, its location in a smart area of Bournemouth and its swimming pool. It was mentioned that my children both went to private school, even though they were subsidised by their grandparents and paid for by the hard work of Gaby and me. The prosecutor must have said more than fifty times that I owned a beautiful Porsche and also offered a lengthy description of Sasha and Nicole playing tennis at the local club.

The prosecutor sought to depict me as a leader of a major fraud that had cost HMRC a calculated sum of £3.8m, stating that in 2008, when Alcatraz's holding company and other firms owned by us went into liquidation, it was all planned by me. When my defending lawyer stated that I was simply obeying British law, which does not treat HMRC for VAT or PAYE as a preferential creditor in the event of liquidation, the prosecution insisted that I had orchestrated the liquidations deliberately, using the tax cash instead to fund a luxurious private lifestyle. The facts show that my brothers and I had invested heavily into our businesses, putting in the money that we all inherited when Father passed away. I personally injected more than £400,000. All three brothers were on modest wages of less than £35,000 per year. With all the hours that we worked, we would have been better off having got jobs working in a supermarket. But all this was to no avail.

HMRC had never attended any of the meetings which all the other creditors attended. It had not asked any questions and had appeared to be satisfied with the liquidation of the companies we were involved with. Eight years later, it had suddenly decided to raise the matter again

VERDICT – GUILTY

By the end of the seven weeks, the jurors were showing signs of frustration and fatigue. I was numb in more than one sense when the verdict came on Tuesday, January 15, 2019, as I had come to the court fresh from a 10.50 am dental appointment to remove my wisdom teeth. I had to drive to Southampton Crown Court, knowing that the jury would soon deliver their verdict. At 2.30 pm, we were called to Court Number 1. The usher asked the foreman to read the verdict.

They had taken only a few hours to re-emerge through the brown prefabricated doors and bring a unanimous verdict for us three brothers and our accountant. I was found guilty on all four counts of defrauding the public revenue and tax evasion, while Shahin, Hedi and Tracy Shaw were each convicted on their one count. Paul Podvoiskis was found not guilty. Judge Henry stated that I was the orchestrator of the deceit and gave us two weeks to clear our affairs before sentencing on February 1, 2019.

During the two weeks before sentencing, while we were sorting out our affairs, I decided to consult another barrister who had represented football manager Harry Redknapp in a similar tax investigation, from which Harry was acquitted. Harry called John Kelsey KC on his private phone while he was on a golf course and told him about our case. It was nice of him. Mr Kelsey immediately asked us to come see him that Thursday in his London office.

My brothers and I went to London and met with Mr Kelsey and his appointed solicitor. We had previously sent them all the paperwork from the court, and after about a one-and-a-half-hour meeting, Mr Kelsey said, 'I wish you had come to see me before the hearing. I can assure you the outcome would have been very different.' Unfortunately, it was too late, and the verdict had already been given. We left his office deeply disappointed.

After returning home, through another friend in a similar position who had also been acquitted, I found another barrister called Miranda Moore KC. After reviewing the paperwork, she advised us the same as Mr Kelsey. Both were well-known barristers who had won many cases against HMRC. I realised that I had made the biggest mistake of my life by not using a proper defence. Going with a law firm that worked with legal aid was a huge mistake. I had thought that since I had done nothing wrong, I shouldn't have to pay for defence. In hindsight, I should have spent as much as I could to get the best defence.

This is my advice to anyone in trouble with HMRC: use the best defence you can. Even if you have to sell your house.

Later, I found out that many criminal lawyers who work with legal aid are always present at police stations on short notice, defending people for petty crimes like theft or fighting. When Berman saw our case and realised the fees involved could be huge, he became my best friend. However, he did not have the capacity, knowledge or right barristers to represent a complex case like ours.

On the first Friday of February, it was snowing as I drove to court with my brothers. On our solicitor's advice, we brought overnight bags. As we approached the Crown Court building, I saw a reporter with a camera and a microphone bearing the BBC logo. Embarrassed, I put my head down and did not answer his questions. In hindsight, I should have spoken my piece. Gaby, Sasha and I entered the courthouse and started looking for Tarquin McCalla, only to learn from Kate Green that he would not be attending, thwarted apparently by the snow.

Later, I found out that he had travelled by train the night before from London to Wiltshire, where his mother lived. He didn't want to drive or take the train from Wiltshire to Southampton because of the snow. However, everyone else – Kate Green, my brothers and I – drove from Bournemouth and surrounding areas to Southampton. What an excuse!

Green said she would ask the judge to postpone the hearing since I did not have a barrister to represent me. The four of us were told to sit at the dock, each with an officer standing behind us. The gallery was full of family and friends, reporters, five HMRC officers and three barristers representing my brothers and the accountant.

Judge Henry began by summarising the convictions. Before he could start, Green rose to ask if the court could be adjourned but Judge Henry quickly shut her down, stating he had made up his mind and would not adjourn the court. I was sentenced to six years in prison, while my brothers received four years each and Tracy Shaw was given a two-year suspended sentence and was asked to leave the court, with an officer ushering her out. The judge was in no doubt. I was 'the power behind the throne; ultimately the orchestrator'.

Sentencing me, he stated, 'I accept that you started this business from virtually nothing and it is a great shame to see somebody like you in court… for these very serious matters. You were convicted by the jury of all four counts that you faced and I have no doubt whatsoever, having heard the evidence, that the emails and other evidence demonstrate that you were in overall charge throughout this cheat on the revenue. You involved others in this fraud by pressure, by persuasion, by force of personality or by playing on the desire of some to keep their jobs.'

HMRC issued a pre-prepared press statement. Spokesman Richard Wilkinson, said: 'The Hashtroudi brothers were serial offenders in setting up businesses and ripping off the British taxpayer, by pocketing the income tax and national insurance contributions employees had paid, and also VAT on sales.'

We were immediately handcuffed by the officers behind us and led through the doors to the stairs to go downstairs. We were each locked up individually in holding cells. There were a few other prisoners locked up, making it very noisy. Six years for financial fraud? An inmate I was later to be imprisoned with would be serving eight years for manslaughter – taking somebody's life. Stunned and shaken, we sought to appeal both the verdict and the sentence but were advised that no judge on the southern England circuit would dare to challenge Judge Henry.

At 5:30 pm, officers led us downstairs in the courts, searched us, and sent us in a wagon to Winchester Prison, where around thirty other prisoners ranging from village simpletons to hardened criminals were awaiting admission to their respective wings. As we walked in, somebody shouted, 'Here are the guys, the mafia from Bournemouth,' likely due to news coverage of our court case.

Although this was hardly the kind of welcome we wanted, our new 'mafia' reputation turned out to work to our advantage during our jail sentence, as rumours spread within the prisons network and we were generally left alone, with other convicts not wanting to mess with a perceived mafia culture. It was not much of a solace.

The grim reality was that 'escaping' from the financial problems of Alcatraz's bars had actually put me behind impenetrable metal ones.

Southampton Crown Court – five of us in the dock

CHAPTER THREE:
NOTHING LIKE PORRIDGE

Norman Stanley Fletcher was wrong. It was not the clanking grey metal door in the grim Victorian confines of HMP Winchester that drove it home for me that my liberty had been lost, my life shattered and my honest reputation ruined. It was Bones, Stud-H, Coolio, Kaggs and Jackson: five heavily tattooed, shaven-headed convicts who threatened me with violence if I did not surrender my bread roll and sparse meat and gravy lunch to them on the first two storeys of the stark metal staircase to my cell. A robust response, a sturdy eye on any waiting crooked legs waiting to trip me up on the steps and a sharp elbow ready to burrow into ribs all became immediately essential for survival. If I lost any of these daily food battles, I might not survive the next week, never mind the whole three years. I wouldn't have anyone as wet behind the ears as Lenny Godber, the naïve cellmate of Fletcher, the habitual criminal famously played by Ronnie Barker in the British TV prison sitcom 'Porridge' as my roomie. Was I really going to be able to survive this?

Before arrival at my new abode, I was called to a room at the courthouse where two officers went through my bag and decided that my white T-shirts and hoodies were not allowed and had to be removed, along with some forbidden toiletries there were not allowed. I repacked what I was allowed and gave the rest to my solicitor to return it to my family. Led by a court officer, I squeezed into a large white Serco van, sitting in the back with no seatbelt or leg room. As the van crawled away from under the courthouse and made its way down the M3, I could see through the darkened windows that the snow was settling. The motorway was completely white.

'THIS PLACE IS FULL OF VERMIN'

When we finally arrived at HMP Winchester, I could see Victorian architecture looming above. The van went through an archway, the front and back gates were locked and an officer wandered around searching under the van with a mirror on a stick. After getting security clearance, we entered a yard and were led one by one into a reception area. I, my brothers and three other prisoners were taken to a dilapidated room where a muscular young Black boy was shouting at a naïve young inmate, who was crying, while another apparently made of sterner stuff was urging the officers to hurry up so that he wouldn't miss his favourite television programme. After our names were called, we headed around a corner to be processed. I was the last one to be summoned and walked hesitantly towards Baldock, an intimidating officer, bald, bearded and replete with tattoos. 'Hashtroudi,' he yelled. 'You got six years. Unluckier than your brothers. Do you understand that?' I replied in the affirmative.

'Are you a calm person?' I shrugged. 'Is this your first time inside?' Yes sir. He turned to another huge officer. 'This place is full of vermin, isn't that right, John?' The giant gave an animalistic grunt. 'Keep your head down and you will be all right.'

Baldock filled in some forms. 'Vultures will soon come knocking,' he advised. 'Say no to everything. You will be fine.' My photo was taken, I was allocated the prison number A2800EH and locked in a holding cell. All the time, I was trying to process what was happening in my head, telling myself that I would be okay, despite plenty of apparent evidence to the contrary. Later I was led out of the cell to a room with two officers sitting on the chair looking right at me. I was told to get naked and perform a squat holding my genitals away from my ass so that the officers could make sure I was not hiding any drugs or weapons up my anus. It was without doubt the most humiliating moment of my life.

That ordeal over, I was told I would not be allowed to wear the tracksuit I had been recommended to bring for my incarceration until I had been inside for a few months without causing trouble. In the meantime, I would have to make do with prison kit. I was handed an over-stretched pair of grey tracksuit bottoms, a standard-issue thick blue prison shirt, three pairs of light blue boxers and some grey thick socks with a hole in them that smelt like someone might have died in them.

Some of the clothes and possessions I had brought with me were put in a bag or stuffed into a prop box, a flimsy black plastic crate that would store everything I was not allowed on the wing. I lost some toiletries, paracetamol and a hardback book which was not permitted in case I used it as a weapon. The £300 I had brought with me in an envelope was taken by an officer with an assurance that it would be added to my account.

Next, I went to the medical room where a uniformed nurse asked if I had any health problems. I said I was fine physically fine. He replied that there would be more checks after the weekend. Another officer fired at me a series of questions. Did I have anything sharp in my pocket, a mental illness or any drugs in my possession. Was I a racist or a homophobe? Had I ever committed arson? Such questions were asked over and over again. Just in case I might change my mind.

THE CURRENCY OF 'STIR'

After declaring that I did not smoke, I was handed a non-smokers pack: a small plastic bag containing a coffee sachet, a biscuit, some melted chocolate and a tiny electric kettle which I was told would cost £10 to replace if I lost or broke it. I asked about visits and was told that I was allowed two per month but had to fill in an application registering visitors' names and addresses for clearance before any visits could start to happen. Handing me a narrow slip of paper containing a PIN number, one officer was firm. 'This is your two-pound emergency phone credit. You can call your close relative in the next 24 hours. You might want to use it now as you won't be out of your cell over the weekend.'

I made my way to a narrow corridor with three battered blue prison payphones on the wall and called Gaby. She had barely uttered the words: 'Hi, how are you, I am fine,' before the credit started plummeting downwards. Was I okay? Yes, I was coping. I just about had enough time to tell her about the visiting rooms and ask after Nicole and Sasha. Gaby started crying. 'Honey, the credit is running out,' I uttered. 'I will say goodbye. Will call you as soon as I can.' I put down the phone and an officer swiftly instructed me to wait for someone to take me to the wing. It felt like the calm before the storm.

My name was called, pointlessly since I was the only person in the room. I picked up my bin liner of belongings and shuffled out, with female officers leading me into a corridor connecting reception to all wings. Spotting my brothers and the young Black prisoner I encountered earlier waiting to be escorted to a wing, I put on a brave smile. About twenty inmates were waiting for other gates so they could go to their individual wings. It seemed that they had just come back from a gym session. Some of them started shouting about the 'Alcatraz mafia' again, which made me uncomfortable. However, at least it meant that officers protected us as we walked to the induction wing.

THE SOUND OF HELL

My abiding memory is the sheer noise. In the book detailing his own imprisonment Chris Atkins writes of "the yelling, banging, screaming, grunting, begging, barking, threatening, ranting, laughing, trading, scoring, whining, arguing, fighting, howling and crying"[1]. I heard them all. It was as if someone had downloaded every single prison sound effect from the internet and was just blaring them out at top volume. Standing on the ground floor of this

---

1   Chris Atkins: "A Bit of a Stretch: The Diaries of a Prisoner (2020)

enormous Victorian edifice, I could see a landing stretching out for 100 yards left and right with blue cell doors running down each wall. Looming above were three more levels with netting between each. Nothing in my life had prepared me for this moment.

I breathed a huge sigh of relief as Hedi and I were escorted to share cell 11D. Shahin was in 12D on his own. Each cell measured 2 m x 3 m and consisted of a sink without a plug hole but with a button to activate the water flow. The toilet was revolting, lacking a seat and sporting stains that made me feel unsafe even when I hovered just above it. There was no screen to provide privacy on the toilet and just about enough room for two metal beds, located next to each other, with a gap of only about 20 cm between them. The mattresses were covered in blue plastic – to facilitate the easy cleaning of body fluid, we were later told. Hedi and I took to our beds, grateful to be together and lay quietly in disbelief. Our only disturbance on that first night, apart from all the noise, was when the cell door was opened by a prison officer to give us stale baguettes wrapped in clingfilm for our dinner. Both were placed unceremoniously in the bin.

On day two, I set about learning the rules of my new life. The phone calls were the first challenge. Each prisoner was given a PIN to which you could add funds, enabling them to make calls to the only people they were cleared to talk to. If the line was engaged or not answered, you had to wait twenty minutes before another attempt was permitted. Only one hour of 'social and domestic' was allowed, so two or three missed calls easily eats up your time for phones calls, showers and speaking to other prisoners.

When officers shouted 'Labour' we had to rush to go to work. Similarly, 'Gym' denoted allotted time in the gymnasium and

'Exercise' meant going to the yard for fresh air. 'Bang up' meant being locked up for long period of time, while 'Segregation' involved isolation, zero privileges and showers and minimal exercise permitted.

My sentence was to be governed by the offender management unit (OMU), staffed mainly by civilians who would plan my courses and jobs. After an initial application, you were assigned a designated OMU manager and a key worker, who you might meet once a month if you were lucky. My first request was a winter jacket, as I was freezing in my cell. Officers (screws) had to be addressed as Mister, with their surname, though most prisoners just called them all Gov. Lady officers had to be called Miss.

No money was available in prison, both on the inside and outside, where the Proceeds of Crime Act (POCA) allowed the government to confiscate assets deemed to be criminal and auction them off. Inside the prison walls, I had an account, to which any earnings from work or small gifts from family could be added to spend in the canteen. Textile jobs paid £9 a week. Trades between prisoners were mostly for possessions or vapes (smoke) but the illegal currency was spice, a dangerous and addictive synthetic version of cannabis, which was popular with prisoners.

INCENTIVES AND PRIVILEGES

With no cash in operation, the incentive and privilege (IEP) system was effectively the currency of imprisonment and one's level was the most important caste. For my first few weeks, I was designated as an 'entry' prisoner, with restricted privileges. Time and good behaviour advanced the level to 'standard' and then, after six to eight weeks, to 'enhanced', where more visits and a higher canteen spend were permitted. Transgressions against prisoners or staff earned negative IEP which could relegate your status.

New prisoners had to undergo 'induction', normally in the first week, where the rules and what courses or what jobs might be available were explained to them. The name and job of each prisoner, together with his picture, were displayed on the left-hand side of each cell door.

Canteen happened every Monday, when a sheet of folder paper with printed items of toiletries and groceries was shoved under your door. You had to fill in the numbers of each item required and hand the form to your landing officer by Wednesday. Canteen items could be collected from a designated office in a sealed clear plastic bag on Fridays.

Enquiries about potential visits or missing groceries in the canteens had to be made on an official application, which had to be submitted to the office of whatever landing you were on. If you were lucky, you might get an answer – and possibly a credit – within a few days, but the decision-makers were not known for their generosity. Medical requests had to be submitted on a different application, with a lengthy wait often resulting for anything not considered urgent.

A CHANGE OF INCARCERATION

Entrance to HMP Dartmoor

After three weeks at Winchester, Hedi was suddenly and without warning told that he was being sent to another category C prison in Coldingley, Surrey, and had one hour to pack his belongings. Despite our attempts to keep him where he was, nobody listened. A few days later, Shahin who had, to his great discomfort, been locked up with Johnson, a stocky, unshaven National Health Service nurse, in jail for abusing a patient, was allowed to join me in his place. We secured jobs as textile workers, making hessian bags for flood barriers. Although the food, security and hygiene were sub-par, we could go to the gym twice a week, providing an opportunity to shower and escape the poor hygiene conditions. Two months later, we were given one hour to pack before being transported to the isolated and distant HMP Dartmoor, on the edge of the famous Devon wilderness. At least we had been allowed to stay together.

At Dartmoor, I was allocated a 2 m by 5 m cell with a very small window, which was broken and had paint peeling off it. Graffiti was on the wall and the light green sheets were adorned with cigarette burns. There was a wash basin with hot and cold tap, a toilet with no seats or privacy screen and a little wooden table and chair. A small television was in the corner.

The concrete floor was covered with worn liner and the light was harsh and fluorescent, despite many attempts by prisoners to cover the brightness with paint or other material. The light made a hissing noise, which would awaken you if officers switched it on from outside so they could see your face. A torch would also be shone from a narrow panel on the cell door, which had a flap that could only be opened and closed from outside. Sometimes officers would leave the light on by mistake. Even if you rang the emergency bell, you were lucky if somebody turned up to switch it off. After a while, I grew used to having to sleep with a bright light on and heavy clunking. The heating was supplied through a four-inch metal pipe running under my bed and was woefully insufficient. The curved bricks on the cell ceiling reminded me of being in a cave.

The shower room smelt of human waste and bleach. It was always steamy and flip-flops were essential, as it was ankle-deep in water, empty shampoo and shower gel, bottles and razors also scattered across the floor. Showers were strictly with pants on and you didn't get long, as the officers would turn off the taps to save water.

After incidents such as fights, 'red regimes' were instituted and we could be locked up for twenty-four hours at a time. The first time this happened was three months into my stay at Dartmoor, when an inmate attempted to commit suicide. He was discovered just in time and placed under observation. We all felt that we were sharing his punishment.

My landing officer was Mr William, an ex-military man, regimental, tall and broad-shouldered, who made it clear from the beginning that he would not tolerate nonsense. He had been at Dartmoor for more than a decade and made sure that I knew it. He was wary of me to begin with but after a few weeks we got on with each other. Rows tended to be trivial and petty. Once, he shouted at me when I was collecting my food. I usually took both a blue plastic bowl and plate to keep separate different types of food, but he told me I had to only use one plate and pile up everything together.

'This is not how I eat my food,' I calmly told him.

'Now you don't eat today,' he shot back, grabbing my plate and shoving it into the trash.

Mr William came to my cell later on and apologised, and he said he had to shout at me in front of others.

'Try to pile up your food from now,' he said, handing me a baguette. I never had any more trouble with him.

On another occasion, I asked Mr William for a mirror. There were none in the cells or shower room as they could be used as a weapon. He reached into his desk and handed me a Perspex mirror the size of a small tile. I thanked him on my return to my cell. Then I needed to stick the mirror to the wall. I went next door to see Nigel, a gnarled seventy-year-old man who had been inside for twelve years for burglary.

'Do you have any glue I can borrow?'

'Toothpaste,' was his reply.

I understood. He wanted to trade. I went back into my cell and came out with a tube of Colgate. Nigel started laughing.

'You idiot. Use the toothpaste to stick the mirror.'

I thought he must be joking but I tried it and it worked. Later, talking to other prisoners, I learned that toothpaste was prison Blu-Tack; used for everything that needed to be stuck. The marketing people at Colgate were clearly missing a trick.

Contact with the outside world could be stressful. Gaby was suffering, having to sell assets to pay the CPS. On one call, she told me the pittance she was being offered for our belongings and I became very upset.

'Why are you accepting low offers?' I yelled. 'I have worked so hard and all my assets are getting sold for nothing.'

It took me a few days to realise that she was right and I was wrong. I was in a bad state of mind. It didn't matter what price she could secure for our possessions; all the proceeds would be going to CPS in any case. I apologised on our next call. With nothing else to think about on such days, running arguments over and again in my head was torture. On another phone call to Gaby, I learned that she had received an offer of £210,000 for one of the flats we owned and had got a letter from the bank asking for repossession of our warehouse and offices.

Then there was the missing out. I missed Sasha and Hannah's wedding on June 22, 2019. I was so sad. Gaby told me it was a beautiful wedding in a lovely church and the reception was at a wonderful venue in a forest. I tried to imagine it and console myself by thinking of the happy couple as they headed to Santorini for their honeymoon. Sasha was offered a new job at a law firm in Southampton later that summer and he flew with Hannah to Johannesburg for a three-week holiday. Nicole went on vacation to Guatemala and the Philippines with her friends from university. I wished I could be with them to share their joy.

Visits could cheer the soul and letters were the highlight of most days. I craved contact with the real world and always replied to everyone who wrote to me. They were my lifeline but they could also be stressful. On one visit, Gaby came together with Shahin's daughter and wife. They came all together and we were not allowed to all sit together. I was not allowed to touch or say anything to my brother's wife or daughter.

BREAKDOWN OF A MARRIAGE

My relationship with Gaby had begun to grow apart a few years before the tax investigation began, due to the stress of running a big business, working long hours and her having to be the best mum in the world on her own, living and breathing for our children. We did not even go to the cinema together any more. We were both devoted: me to my work, her to the children.

Unfortunately, the stress of my trial, conviction and imprisonment became too hard for Gaby to bear and by September she had told me that she was filing for divorce. Of course, I was very saddened about this, after all our happy years together. But it was going to be a very long three years and I had to understand.

In prison, everyone used to say when you went back home after a few years, your wife might have new habits. When one fellow prisoner was released after many years, he discovered that his old marital tradition of attending a pub quiz night with his wife every Tuesday had been ended during his incarceration. She now went to yoga instead. Many other habits had also changed and they could not live together.

Fortunately, Stavy Antoniou, a friend with whom I had long shared ideas about life and business, stayed in touch. She had been for many years a customer in one of our restaurants, I knew her family well and we had exchanged ideas and become close, training together at the gym we both attended. When I told her that the divorce would mean I did not have an address for the prison to eventually release me to, she said I could stay in her house. After this, we realised that our feelings for each other amounted to more than just friendship and became romantically involved.

Stavy sent me a book for meditation and diary to keep me occupied by writing about my daily routine, but when I went to reception to collect it, an officer refused to release it.

'This has a martial arts context and is not allowed,' he said gruffly, putting the gifts back into my confiscated property box. Little things like this made and broke my days inside.

At Dartmoor, Shahin and I found jobs in textiles, making trousers for prisoners, which allowed us to work five days a week. Hedi and I corresponded by letters and I managed to get permission to phone him twice with an officer present in the room. Once, we were even allowed to converse in Persian.

Otherwise, life at the prison was humdrum and I took every opportunity to try to break the boredom. In August, I went along to a meeting of the Dialogue Road Map (DRM), a training scheme provided by an individual contractor offering one-on-one counselling and mediation to inform prisoners' attitudes to life and help them navigate their relationships and communicate with their families. The meeting was on E-Wing but I very nearly missed it as officers found a weight missing in the gym while I was training there. The gym was immediately locked down and nobody could leave until the weight had been found. After about an hour, it was discovered stashed underneath a cycling saddle. It made me miss my lunch and I only just made it to the DRM meeting. The training sounded really positive and something I really wanted to do. I put in an application.

Later that month, I was on a treadmill in the gym when an officer asked me to follow him to a room where they took a urine test for drugs. It was difficult to pass urine after being on a treadmill for a while, but I managed it in the end and the test came back negative. I later discovered that the check was connected to my application for a position on the DRM job. It was a high-security job, paying £25 pounds a week and came with the privilege of a security pass allowing me to visit inmates in every wing. The prison wanted to make sure I was not using drugs. Fortunately, this was something I never did, even when it was all around me.

I had to tell my boss in the textiles operation that I had applied for a DRM job. He was not happy, especially as he was also losing Bruno, an Italian prisoner who was being released and going home after a decade inside. I was accepted for the DRM job but was less successful with an application for an accountancy course with software group Sage. Due to my conviction for fraud, I was banned from studying accountancy. One step forward, one step back.

LEARNING TO LISTEN

The DRM course began in September led by Maria Arpa, a distinguished and determined lady who had been honoured with an MBE. There was a lot to learn and I found it very exciting. She trained us every morning from 8:15 am, with a break for lunch. Then we were back at it from 1:45 pm to 4.30 pm. The course lasted two months. Then, from November, I was allowed to start processing DRM applications and conducting one-to-one sessions with inmates as well as groups with eight to ten prisoners from different wings. For one-on-one sessions, there always had to be two facilitators present for our safety and there was a bell in case of any problems. Everything I learned in the sessions was confidential and I was not allowed to discuss it with any officer, unless I thought the prisoner involved was going to hurt himself or hurt others or commit suicide.

There were also still legal matters to attend to. Stavy was trying to find a solicitor and a barrister to appeal against my conviction, and then Maria Arpa gave me the name of a London solicitor called Hesham Puri who said he would help with my case. He instructed a barrister called Jeffrey Israel to take the case to a court of appeal. It would cost £30,000, which Gaby and Stavy agreed to finance. This made me really happy and I broke the news to Shahin. Now I had to wait and see. It might take a year but it gave me hope. I wrote to Kate Green, stating that I had lost confidence in the firm and I wanted Hesham to handle my case from now on.

What a year! And it ended with a bang. Returning to my cell after work on December 30, an officer slammed the door on my hand. My fingers went black and my hand was bleeding. I was not even allowed to see a nurse. I was in agony and we were to be locked up until January 2. It was not a happy New Year.

CHAPTER FOUR:
761 DAYS TO FREEDOM

Disaster struck on the second day of 2020 when I learned I was being transferred back to Winchester Prison for a 'proceeds of crime' hearing at Southampton Crown Court. I had begged for a video link session and thought it had been approved but was suddenly told to pack my things. It wasn't the actual hearing I was worried about. Changes of prison are traumatic events. Everything you have built is lost; all trust disappears. You have to start again with no privileges. Winchester was also a tougher prison, graded B, compared to Dartmoor's C. This was truly terrible news.

The Serco van to transport me arrived at Dartmoor at 8 am on a Friday and arrived at Winchester by 2 pm. I asked the officer who did my transfer how much it was costing the taxpayer and he said it was about £3,000. It was 7.30 pm before I was allocated cell 35 on the fourth floor of C Wing. I was given no food all day. It felt like one of the worst days of my life. My new cell was dirty but at least it was a single. I had to tell a nurse that I suffered from irritable bowel syndrome in order to be able to pull off that one. There was no table, chair or television and the tap locked after I pressed it five times. There was no water for forty minutes. It took a day to get a TV from another prisoner. I was allowed to take a shower and then locked up again. It was a very difficult time.

Some prisoners would block their sink and turn on the taps until they flooded the cell in order to get attention from the officers. For this reason, the taps would only work for a small amount of time. On pressing them a few times, they would stop altogether for forty minutes for so-called 'security' reasons.

The next day, I was told I had only five minutes to collect my lunch, due to a 'spice problem'. All C Wing was locked and it felt a very unsafe environment, with all the officers wearing riot gear and masks. It looked like a scene from a Mad Max movie and it was freezing in the cell, while screws patrolled the stairs and landings with dogs. By Monday, I had still not been allowed a shower and again had only five minutes to collect my food. My court hearing was the next day. I looked a mess and felt dirty. It felt terribly degrading and the noise was so bad that I couldn't even sleep.

UNHEARD AT A HEARING

At 8 am on the Tuesday, I was transferred to Southampton court for a hearing back before Judge Henry.

'Your honour,' I said, when I was allowed to speak, 'I wrote to you asking if I could attend this hearing through a video link but I never heard back. I had a job in Dartmoor, I was familiar with my surroundings there and I have been staying out of trouble.'

'Yes,' he replied. 'I received your letter and I told my clerk that there was no need for you to be transferred but somehow the message didn't go through. But now you're here.'

I was so close to telling him to say that to someone who really cared, but I somehow held back. The hearing was only for legal directions to be given and it would be another few months before another proceeds of crime hearing and a separate session for my divorce. I was taken downstairs to the same courtroom cells where my prison journey started nearly a year before. At 5 pm, I was taken back to HMP Winchester after another day with no food or drink.

My new home was in another building in cell S2-11. It was another single and decent-sized cell boasting larger windows. To my astonishment, it contained a telephone on which I could call my family with my PIN at any time of the day. It felt like a miracle; a freezing cold one, since there would be no electricity until midday the following day. As I cleaned my cell and started to settle in, I was given fish and chips and an apple. None of the officers knew when I would be transferred back to Dartmoor. I missed my brother.

A week later, there was a massive fight. Sean, a middle-aged, dark-haired, fidgety, languid prisoner had been experiencing issues with a group of inmates on another wing. After many days of experiencing constant goading, he blew a fuse and threw hot water over them, leading to three people having to be admitted to hospital with burns. Ten inmates were involved in the brawl and a revenge attack was anticipated. My cell was the closest to the entrance. I just hoped I wouldn't get embroiled in the backlash.

Gaby visited and told me that two of the property sales had fallen through. She cried for the entire visit. It didn't feel good and by 5 pm I was back in my cell, with the wing shut down on code red due to the fight. The next day there was no heating. I was desperate to go back to Dartmoor but it looked like another fight was looming.

Amazingly, at 6 am on one day two weeks later an officer rapped on my cell door and ordered me to get ready. The move was actually happening. A van collected me at 11.30 am and delivered me back at HMP Dartmoor nearly five hours later. I had to go through the entire reception process again but I didn't care. By 6 pm, I was banged up in cell D5-11. Twelve hours after I was moved to G-Wing: no G4-37.

MOVING TO THE LIFEBOAT

Soon afterwards, I was informed that, after many letters of request, I was to be moved to E-Wing, a small section that was much quieter and home to only fifty mostly older inmates.

Many of them were working for DRM on privileges and were unlikely to be unruly. The showers were better and safer too.

Prisoners called E-Wing the 'lifeboat'. I was finally moved there on February 12. I got a small, very dirty cell, with a metal toilet with no seat, but it didn't matter. At least I was there. I hoped I could stay there until my release. I went back to work as a DRM facilitator. On many occasions, I requested different officers to allow for my brother to be moved to E-Wing. Luckily, he was finally moved one month before me.

Legal tussles continued. Gaby and her solicitor went to court to stop proceedings for the repossession of our warehouse and the offices, but the judge made an order giving just two more weeks to find a buyer. Gaby had no alternative but to accept a reduced price. In February, I was advised on a video call with Hesham Puri and Jeffrey

Israel that my appeal could go ahead, though there was a very slim chance of a positive result. I decided to go ahead. On my return to my cell, I was told that to my request for transfer to a lower-security D category prison has been denied, without explanation. I was painfully aware of the family events I was missing: Sasha's holiday in the Maldives; the second anniversary of the death of Gaby's father. As the divorce proceedings rumbled on, my twenty-ninth wedding anniversary clashed with a proceeds of crimes final hearing in court in Southampton. A friend called Jim sadly passed away.

A DIFFERENT KIND OF LOCKDOWN

Then came Covid. It started with all the officers and inmates being issued with facemasks and gym sessions reduced to a smaller number of inmates, with each machine cleaned after use.

In March, as Prime Minister Boris Johnson ordered the closure of all restaurants and pubs, most jobs in UK prisons were also suspended. We were to be banged up all day, with only twenty minutes for showers and ten minutes for phone calls until further notice. All exercise was moved outdoors. All visits were stopped. Even a video interview with Hesham Puri about my appeal was cancelled. At the end of March, I received a letter stating that my appeal could take another five months before it got in front of any judge. Luckily, the proceeds of crime hearing was cancelled, so I would not have to be transferred to HMP Winchester again. Hedi was not so fortunate. I learned by letter that he had caught Covid and was placed in isolation.

In April, I slipped while running in the prison yard and hurt my leg. I could barely walk. Some inmates tested positive for Covid positive in F and D wings and eight prisoners were moved from E to B Wing to make space for quarantine. A week later, the 6.30 am move cycle began again. Luckily, I was only moved downstairs. The cell was cold and the water didn't work. A few days later, I was moved again, to E2-22. At this rate, I would experience every single inch of this prison. I tested negative for HIV and hepatitis.

From home, I learned that Stavy had moved all my clothes to her flat. Day fifty of prison lockdown was Stavy's birthday. My old family house had been put up for sale. Hedi was moved to HMP Ford, a category D open prison, which made me very happy.

During Ramadan, we were allowed to request Halal food and to go to pray, but, as Shahin and I are not practising Muslims, we did neither. A polite young Muslim priest came to our cell, asked how I was and delivered holy literature, which I found fascinating. Anything to lift the monotony.

On day seventy of prison lockdown, my DRM sessions started again, though my first one was cancelled due to my client Russ Bishop, a rough-looking, unkempt man who always had dirt in his fingernails, getting into a fight and being placed in segregation. On day 103, the government ordered the re-opening of all UK pubs and restaurants. I appealed again to be allowed to move to a category D jail. Again, it was refused. I received a letter reference my appeal against the decision of me moving to D category and again, they declined it for the second time with no given reason. On day 125, I learned that Sasha had a new, better-paid job at a solicitors' firm in Southampton.

Grave matters were proceeding. On day 127 of lockdown,

which was also Sasha's birthday, I connected to a video hearing at Southampton Crown Court where Judge Henry ordered

£339,000 pounds to be paid as proceeds of crime within three months. If we could not find the money, he would add another four years to my prison sentence. As Gaby owned 50 percent of our house and there was a mortgage and second bank charge for the bank to be paid, it was not going to be easy to find this money. I tried to call Gaby and Sasha but both were not available. On day 157 of lockdown at Shahin's final proceeds of crimes hearing, Judge Henry ordered him to pay £530,000 within three months. Everything would have to be sold, with the proceeds paid to the CPS. Shahin would have nowhere to go when released. He was inconsolable.

A MATTER OF RACE

I was given a worrying new neighbour on E-Wing. David Norris was serving a life sentence for the racially motivated murder of Black teenager Stephen Lawrence. Being clearly of Middle Eastern origin, I feared the worst and to begin with, Norris would not even acknowledge me. Then, one day I was waiting for Shahin before collecting my food when Norris joined the queue and I motioned for him to pass me. After that, he began talking to me every day. He worked in the gardens and occasionally joined DRM circle discussions. We seemed to get on okay. On day 162 of lockdown, another new prisoner arrived a few cells down from me. Fred was serving six years for abuse of stepchildren. He was appealing against his conviction, claiming that the real father was instead the abuser. This was prison life. Nobody there was ever guilty.

On day 175 of lockdown, it was six months since I saw any of my family or Stavy. The prison said it would set up video calls to family and friends, with each prisoner permitted two per month. On day 180, Gaby exchanged contracts today on a flat I owned in Camberley and moved into rented accommodation with Nicole. On day 191, she also exchanged on our offices and warehouse. My request to transfer to a category D prison was refused again.

Some good news finally arrived on day 197 of lockdown when Sasha told me that Hannah was pregnant and I was going to be a grandfather. Then Gaby's mother suffered a fall and she was taken to the hospital. Gaby was devastated. My former family house was finally sold. I was devastated. I loved that house.

Things in prison could always get worse. On October 22, the spectre of the 6.30 am cell move arose again and this time I was being moved to A-Wing, one of the worst parts of Dartmoor. Only five prisoners were being kept on E-Wing to carry out daily functions like laundry. My job in the DRM meant I had to move. Shahin agreed to take a laundry job so he could stay safe on E-Wing, which was safer for him but there was no escape for me. A-Wing consisted of five floors housing nearly 180 prisoners. Renowned as a noisy, feisty, boisterous wing, with a lot of fights, it was mostly full of young inmates, looking for trouble.

I was put into a cell on the fifth floor, a few doors down from an Irish prisoner called Brian who I worked with in the DRM. A short, chubby man with a round face, he was forty years old, had been in and out of prison since he was fourteen and knew how the system worked. Now that we were both in a same wing, we would be conducting most of the one-to-one DRM sessions together.

One month and a day after moving to A-Wing, I was collecting my food when a prisoner in front of me suddenly collapsed and died. Apparently, he suffered a stroke. We were all banged up until a medic arrived.

The last month of my first full calendar year inside passed slowly and painfully. My cell was unbearably cold. Looking out from the window, I could see snow on Dartmoor's hills. Some of the staff were snowed in, so we were placed under the red regime most of the time. Covid wasn't helping either, with 137 inmates on A-Wing testing positive. Soon it was 138 as I tested positive too. Two nurses put a sticker on my cell and I was confined to my cell. This would be my regime for the next few weeks. Every two or three days, I would get my rubbish collected and handed a mobile phone for a ten-minute call to family. I could only shower once every three days and for ten minutes only.

What a Christmas. Later that day, my cell door opened and an officer yelled at me to step back. He put a sandwich on the floor, kicked it towards me and then locked the door. You would not even treat a dog in this way.

CHAPTER FIVE:
FROM PRISONER TO
COUNSELLOR

Eight days into 2021, the sticker was removed from my door and I was out of Covid isolation. A week later, however, I was plunged into a different kind of despair when my appeal was refused. I was devastated. Returning to my wing, I bumped into Dave Woolley, an orderly from the gym. Extremely tough, with neck tattoos and bulging muscles, he was the head of the Hells Angels in the south-west. When I asked how he was, he told me his son had just told him that his mother had died of Covid. He was inconsolable too. Later in January, I led a DRM session with Dave to help him to deal with his grief on his mother's passing. He was extremely emotional.

Another prisoner, a young guy called Marcus was suffering mental health problems and lost it one day, screaming at the top of his voice. Three officers jumped on him, beat him up and then tossed him in the safe cell, where a prisoner is watched twenty-four hours a day, seven days a week. Even his trips to the toilet were supervised. He should have been in a mental institution, not a prison. It was not fair to treat him like that.

Separately, an inmate I was having DRM sessions with attempted to commit suicide. He survived but was put onto constant watch in another safe cell. Despite all the work we do with inmates on DRM, we never know what they are going to do next.

Family news was, as ever, a mixed bag. At the end of the month, I managed to go and see Shahin on E-Wing. Lucky Shahin. He was getting ready to be released the following day, when Hedi would also be released from HMP Ford. Their two years were up but I had another year to serve. I would be on my own now. In February, Gaby's mother had her toe amputated, due to her fall. On February 23, I was connected by video for my divorce hearing. A judge finalised the proceedings and I received all the paperwork by the end of the week.

My job in the DRM was changing too. Brian resigned, deciding that listening to other peoples' problems was not for him. I had to find another facilitator to accompany me in my sessions, but the prison also had a new governor, a Mr Mead, who was reluctant to continue funding the scheme due to cost concerns. As he pontificated, many of the DRM staffers, including me, began to think that we needed to look for other jobs as DRM might not exist for much longer. As the old saying goes, in prison things change on a daily basis until you get used to it.

A NEW JOB

At the end of March, I started a new job as a newspaper orderly with Mark Butcher, a tall, broad-shouldered lorry driver serving seven years who I knew from E-Wing. We had an office to ourselves, organising the newspapers and magazines for the entire prison. Prisoners placed orders, which we processed on a computer, sending the details to the accounts department to deduct the money from each prisoner. It was a nice job and for the moment I had two positions as the governor had asked us to resume with the DRM.

My days started to go by faster. I needed to finish my sentence. Gaby's mother fell from her wheelchair, cut her forehead and suffered two black eyes. She needed four stitches. I was most upset that I could not be there to help. In April, Gaby rang to remind me that we got married exactly thirty years ago. Even though we were now divorced, we remained very good friends, perhaps even closer than we were before sometimes. On April 17, we were locked up at 10.30 am so everyone could watch Prince Philip's funeral. At 5:11am one day in May, my grandson was born in Dorchester Hospital. Around the same time, I learned that my request to be transferred to a category D, or 'open' prison, had been rejected again. Apparently, I was considered to be high-risk in an open environment. Prison was indeed a jumble of life, death and being unable to escape oneself.

Counselling other prisoners sometimes put my own situation into perspective. Four cells away from my cell there was an Italian called Marchello. Whenever we had a chance, we spoke to each other as the only foreigners on our floor. After a long time, he began to trust me and told me about his life story. He shared that when he was eleven years old the mafia took him to a cave and gave him a vest to wear before shooting him three times. He didn't realise that the vest was bullet-proof vest, so assumed he was about to die. He survived due to the vest, an initiation test to see if he was brave enough. Marchello worked for the mafia until he was eighteen, then joined the Italian army.

After military service, he came to Britain, working as a washer-upper at an Iranian restaurant. Not wishing to return to Italy and his mafia life, he became a British train driver, got married and divorced and had a daughter, then nineteen, who was studying at university in the UK while his eighty-eight-year-old mother continued to live in Italy. Like most prisoners, Marchello never told me why he was in prison, but said that once his sentence was over, he would be deported to Italy and wanted to live with his mother in Italy. We talked about Italian food every day and he said he would send me recipes when we were both released.

There was more trouble on A-Wing, with a fight setting off the alarm. Mr Thai, a surly, grimacing officer with menacing eyes who was widely disliked, had been reprimanding a prisoner who retaliated, giving him a black eye and biting his ear. We were all sent to our cells while other officers grabbed the inmate and threw him into segregation. Bang went that night's shower and phone calls.

STAY OF EXECUTION

In April, the governor announced that he would keep running DRM until at least the end of September. While the job came with a badge entitling me to enter all of the prison's wings and go to the gym every day outside lockdowns. It had its downsides too. One was the opportunity it provided to deliver contraband or illicit messages for inmates. I always declined such requests. If you got caught, you would lose your job, badge and privileges. It simply was not worth it. Eventually, prisoners realised that I would never agree to do it and stopped asking.

Sometimes inmates asked me for help personally. Neil, who lived a few doors down from my cell, asked me to mediate with the family of a young man who he had stabbed and killed. The victim's family wanted to visit his killer and speak to him. I told Neil that I could prepare him but was not allowed to hold a DRM session with the victim's family as they lived outside of the prison. We ran a few sessions with Neil and prepared him for the visit when the victim's parents wanted to know exactly what had happened and if he had any remorse. Neil was serving a life sentence. He told the parents that he was sorry and that what had happened was a madness that he had never intended. He asked whether they could ever forgive him and, on their last visit, the mother said that she had. Being part of this restorative justice process was incredibly rewarding for me and it was great too to see the relief that it brought to all the parties, including Neil himself.

Then there was a DRM session with Oliver, a prisoner who had been on his wing for years and had always kept himself to himself, never wanting to speak about his crime. He suddenly broke his silence, telling me that he stood on the head of his newborn baby to shut him up from crying, killing the infant. It was heavy stuff but I told him that I thought he was ready to do more sessions and to try to move forward. I persuaded Oliver to start exercising in the gym, where sessions had finally been brought back indoors, and to enrol for education. After about a year, he was moved to another prison. I hope he is doing well.

Brian was released on licence in May, on condition that he lived at an approved address. I hoped that he would stay out of trouble and make a new life for himself, having been in and out of prison for twenty-eight years. Then forty-two, he was clearly institutionalised. Indeed, he revealed that after a previous release he had found a job at a takeaway joint but had developed a drinking problem and flouted his curfew restrictions to go to pubs. He was given a warning, returned to his address and fell asleep, but the following morning he decided that he would be better off back in prison where he wouldn't have to work and wouldn't be able to drink. He went to the nearest police station, handed himself over, telling a surprised officer that he had broken his curfew and deserved to be sent back to jail. When the duty sergeant replied that he did not have the power to send Brian back to prison, he went out to buy a litre of petrol, took it to a nearby church and set fire to the door. He then duly called the police, who arrested him. for arson and sent him back to prison. What a waste of humanity.

'I used to feel at home in prison,' he told me, 'but I have grown up and now feel different.'

I gave Brian some books about Hinduism and Buddhism. He loved reading them and borrowed similar books from the prison library. He told me that his ambition on his latest release was to go and practise Buddhism and that he felt ready. Only time will tell, I thought to myself. I still have no idea how he is faring.

In my own restorative justice process, Judge Henry finally reduced my proceeds of crime repayment to £202,500. Back on the wing, I was trying to phone Stavy to tell her when a fight started in the queue, with a man called Baylee starting to beat another prisoner called Harry Potter, who was said to have changed his name multiple times so that nobody could find out his crime. The talk was that he was a sex offender, though he was not on that wing. I never knew. He was certainly a strange-looking skinny man who would avoid making eye contact even when talking to somebody. I was kind of grateful that he had not sought to confide in me through the DRM process. How would I have been able to help him?

In June, Greco, a young man from Christchurch in Dorset, was told by an officer to return to his cell. When he refused, five officers beat him up, kicked him on the floor and then put him in segregation. There was no need for that and we all suffered consequences. I was told by an officer to cut my phone call short and get back to my cell.

DOING BIRD

The following month, a seagull became stuck in the barbed wire on top of the prison walls and officers called in the RSPCA to help. Prisoners began screaming that a mere seagull was getting more attention than a prisoner in A-Wing and a mini-riot kicked off, although the flames were soon put out by riot officers. The incident ended predictably with the seagull freed and all the rest of us locked down under a red regime. Franz Kafka would have had a field day with that story.

Another DRM session involved a young lad named Jeff who was moved into the cell next to mine. Brought up in a respectable family, he told me he got bored one day, dressed up in a suit, paid a taxi driver nearly £100 to take him to a forest and he tried to hang himself from a tree. A branch gave in and he fell unconscious to the ground, where he was found by a farmer and taken to hospital.

Jeff survived but seemed to deal with his inner rage by abusing his girlfriend and was now in prison. He told me his sister had just told him that she had decided to have a sex change. He felt devastated and suicidal but the session seemed to help greatly. I do hope that he is all right.

Neil, who lived on the fourth floor of A-Wing a few doors down from me, had a stroke one morning and was transferred to hospital. Elsewhere, Cooper, who I had previously run DRM sessions for, was committed to a mental hospital as he was considered unsafe in prison due to self-harm and suicide attempts. A new prisoner who was working at the stores stopped me on my way to the wing one day and asked if he could schedule a DRM session. He told me he was serving nineteen years for a murder that he committed in ten minutes of madness and he did not know if he could cope with prison life.

Another disclosure came in a DRM when a prisoner confided that he had been raped by his father at the age of seven years and that his dad also raped his sister. The father was put in prison and his mother found a new boyfriend, but both children were abandoned as teenagers. No wonder this inmate had ended up in jail. Some of these stories made me weep inside.

In August, Hedi told me he had received a letter stating that bailiffs would be sent to his house because of non-payment of business rates for our former warehouse and offices. He didn't know what to do. I told him to leave it to me. Later I called Stavy and asked her to call the business rates office and tell them of our situation. She did exactly that and the council withdrew its summons. Even in prison, I still had to do work for others.

After gym and a shower, we usually had to wait for an officer to open the gates so we could go back to our wings. One day while I was waiting, a prisoner with a large head and patchy skin on his face looked at me and said hello in Portuguese. I found out he was Brazilian and asked where in the prison he lived. He didn't understand me and the only English word he seemed to know was 'help'. When he said it, I didn't understand what he wanted and we had to leave the gym but later I found him easily on A-Wing. With the aid of a dictionary, he said he was from San Paulo and was serving a nineteen-year sentence. He told me he suffered mental health difficulties, felt he was being isolated and didn't understand what people wanted from him. I managed to get him into a DRM session with the help of Mr Middleton, our previous officer.

It turned out that he was doing time for a murder in Bristol. He had been a fisherman in Brazil, married with two sons, but could not make ends, so came to England and found a job in a takeaway, sending his pay back to Brazil for his wife and the children's education. After a while, he lent a Brazilian colleague £2,000, but when he asked to be repaid, the man denied all knowledge of the loan. The first man became angry and threatened his compatriot at work with a kitchen knife. A struggled ensured and he stabbed the borrower three times, killing him. He was arrested, pleaded guilty verdict and was sent to Dartmoor after two years at HMP Bristol. He told me he was devastated by his crime, had suffered poor mental health and had not been able to communicate with anyone.

'You're the first person to ever understand me,' he told me. I wrote a letter to the Brazilian consulate explaining his situation. A few weeks later, we received a reply that the consulate had managed to communicate to his family in Brazil. The consulate also got in touch directly with HMP Dartmoor's governor and a lady called Hazel, who worked for Home Affairs, came to see him. Hazel organised for someone to come in once a week to teach him English and he ended up with a regular phone calls to his wife and his sons. The man said he was having these dreams of a spirit coming to him and touching him. I recommended that he see a mental health practitioner and arranged for a meeting to be scheduled with a meeting with the doctor and psychologist.

'STASHING THE HOOCH'

My DRM work did not exclude me from suspicion, however. On the contrary, as I was doing the paper runs one day in August, an officer accosted me in a corridor and asked me to follow him to my cell where two other officers were going through my belongings, pulling apart my mattress and pillow. Outside the cell, I was asked where I was 'stashing the hooch'. I told them I don't know what hooch was. I had no idea it was an illegal drink made by prisoners in their cells from lemon or orange peel and sugar and fermented for thirty days. When I asked why the officer thought I was concocting this drink, he replied that my cell always smelt of orange. I took him to the radiator in my cell and showed him how I put orange peel on the pipe to make the cell smell nicer. He told me to immediately stop doing that. The officers could not find anything but still locked me up for the whole day and it took me all afternoon to put my cell back in order. They could have saved a lot of time and trouble by asking me before ransacking my cell.

Bad news seemed to come in batches. On August 28, Gaby's mother passed away at 7:30 am in a Swiss care home. I was devastated. I loved her dearly. She had been like a mother to me. Soon afterwards, I received a reply to a letter I had written to letter to Judge Henry, pleading for early release as I had been doing good work in prison. True to that judge's form, he refused my request. Later, I had to join Judge Henry in another court session via video session to resolve a discrepancy that had arisen in his confiscation order. The figure had been miscalculated, it transpired, by the princely sum of 75p. I could not believe that a duty barrister was having to represent me against a prosecution silk for such a paltry sum. What a waste of taxpayers' money. The hearing was concluded in fifteen minutes. Even that was a complete waste of time

Peter Drummond, who was serving eight years, used to be a policeman in the anti-terrorist squad but started a relationship with a fifteen-year-old girl, was caught and was now divorced with two children and serving eight years on A-Wing. He asked for a one-to-one DRM session. So did Louis, a twenty-eight-year-old white male who said he got into drug dealing, learning everything from his mother, who was a dealer herself. They were now both in prison. Another applicant was Aki, a skinny twenty-nine-year-old Ethiopian asylum-seeker who had been living in Wales. He had got into university to study politics but went to a club one night, got drunk and took a girl he met there back to her place. The next morning, he was arrested for rape. He was found guilty at trial and sentenced to eight years.

COUNSELLING THE COUNSELLORS

Sometimes us counsellors needed help too. Tim, who I worked with in leading DRM sessions together, was devastated when he received news that his father had been diagnosed with pancreatic cancer. He carried on providing help for prisoners without mentioning his own situation.

On October 21, only 102 days of my sentence remained but the prison system still had surprises up its sleeve. I was informed that I was being transferred that day to HMP Channings Wood. I protested, asking if anything could be done to keep me at Dartmoor so close to my release date. I would have no job there at the Devon prison and it would be difficult to settle into a new jail for such a short time. My protests were to no avail. The governors had made their decision. A new law apparently stated that the last three months of all UK prison sentences had to be served in what was deemed to be a 'local prison'.

I had no choice. I was locked up for the evening, taken to reception at 8:15 the next day to collect my belongings and slotted into a Serco van to take me and a few others to our new temporary home. We left Dartmoor at midday and arrived at our destination at 2:30 pm.

Following the usual reception procedures, I was transferred to the induction wing. Luckily, I had a single cell including a shower. The cell was dirty but comparatively spacious, the sun shone through the large windows more than in any of my previous captive abodes and – luxury upon luxury – for the first time in my imprisonment I had a shower in my cell. I was still unhappy. Serving time was the hardest experience I had ever endured in my life and even towards the end it seemed to have more difficulties in store for me. I had a new environment, different neighbours and a whole new set of potential problems to navigate. It was going to take time to settle in. The new law deserved to be cursed.

Seven days later, I was moved again to a new building at Channings Wood called LB3. This place was worse than Winchester, with prisoners constantly shouting, crying and fighting. In my first few days there, I saw more fights than in two years at Dartmoor. My new cell was tiny, with a large window and along the hallway there was a dirty shower with water up to your ankles. It was the filthiest place I had seen.

A month passed before I was moved again, this time to cell LB2-2.36 on the enhanced wing. The cell was so dirty that it took me the whole day to clean it. A chubby Black man called Nelson told me which was the best shower and I met my new next-door neighbour Richard, a thirty-six-year-old who had spent most of his life serving short sentences for theft. This time, he was inside for six years for stabbing somebody.

Richard had a habit of throwing his rubbish out of the window into the yard, infuriating the prisoner who cleaned it and swore every morning that he would kill the perpetrator if he ever met him. Dangerously, the would-be murderer did not know whether the culprit was Richard or me as he was confused about which window the rubbish came down from. I pleaded with God to help us both.

Most of the times a fight happened, I kept myself to myself, but one day while I was walking in the yard, a tall, clean-looking London prisoner called Gavin started talking to me. He heard what I was serving time for – something I was told never to do in prison – and told me he had every sympathy for me. Emboldened by his breach of this unwritten rule, I asked him the same question. He told me that a friend serving a sentence in another wing owed him £12,000. When he was asked to pay up, this pal told Gavin that he had invested the money in hashish from Morocco and would repay him with 50 kg of the drugs. Gavin accepted the deal on the basis that it would at least give him back his capital. But all this communication took place on mobile phones that had been tapped by the police. Both men's houses were raided, their phones seized and their messages unencrypted, convicting each of them. They were each serving three-year prison sentences. Gavin told me the cost of hashish in Morocco is £8 per kilo but it can fetch £350 per kilo in Britain.

FOOD AND MEDICINE

Before I was sent to prison, I hated to take any medication, often quoting Apple co-founder Steve Jobs' comment that food should be one's medicine. Yet now I had no choice; prison food was so poor in nutrients. In November, I was called to healthcare after a blood test showed a deficiency of vitamin B12 injection because of my jailbird diet. More jabs had to follow every two days.

I also used to not watch much television either, but inside prison there is little else to do. At Channings Wood, the must-watch programme was a Channel Five documentary about one of the prison's residents, a grey-haired ex-prison resident who had lived on several wings before being released, He was recaptured in Spain, living a lavish life with yachts, ladies and lucrative earnings from drugs. Everybody at Channings Wood except for me knew all about him.

Waiting in a queue for the phone in December, I sat next to a man of about seventy-five years who very much resembled a woman, with long grey hair. I asked Gavin who he was and he told me to be careful; it was a gay man who had stabbed and killed his boyfriend while both were serving prison sentences. He had fallen in love and had a relationship with the inmate a year before his partner was due to be released. When the time came, he entered his cell and stabbed him fifty times, saying he did not want him to be released and to be left all alone in prison.

'That guy should be on a psychiatric ward, not in a prison,' I told Gavin. 'There are some seriously scary people here.' The homosexual issue was puzzling. A widespread preconception in the outside world is that when men go to prison, they either get raped or are forced to perform sexual favours. In fact, over my three years of imprisonment, I did not once see or hear of a sexual act. There were inmates who consensually fell in love with each other but, in my experience, the sexual expression in prisons that one sees in movies seldom occurs in British jails. Whenever I took a shower, there was a line of ready potential witnesses to any unwanted encounter whose only thought was their own cleansing. The time granted to shower was minimal and the shower doors were always locked. If cell doors were left open, one was more likely to get beaten up by an officer than sexually abused. Those were the facts in the prisons where I was an unwilling guest of Her Majesty.

LAST CHRISTMAS

My final Christmas in prison was by far my worst, virtually locked in my cell for the duration of the holiday season. On January 3, 2022, Gavin gave me his prison jacket and bid me goodbye as he was being released. I needed it as the weather was bitter. The gym at Channings Wood was very small and, due to Covid, I only used it twice. I put my head down and spent most days in my cell locked up, knowing that I would soon be a free man. The day before my release, I donated my Nike running shoes to the hardest man in the servery, who bore frightening tattoos on his neck and forehead. He had always given me extra bread, so this was his reward.

When my release day of January 31 finally dawned, there was inevitably a delay. Normally, prisoners due for release are taken to reception by 7:30 am, processed by 9 am and out of the gate pretty soon afterwards, but due to staff shortages, my release did not happen until 12:30 pm. When the moment finally arrived, an officer took me through the gates and I found Stavy waiting for me outside. I had been anxious about what would happen when I left prison as I had nowhere to live, but Stavy offered to let me stay with her on the south coast until I got myself sorted. We later became romantically involved and now share our lives.

We had to drive from Devon to Dorset and needed to check in with my probation office by 3 pm. It did not feel like much of a constraint. It was a dream come true. I told Stavy to drive quickly, before anyone at the prison changed their mind. At last I was free.

PART TWO:
FROM TABRIZ TO PERSEPOLIS

CHAPTER SIX:
THE WHOLE WORLD IS WHITE

In the still, pre-dawn hours of late 1950s Tehran, my childhood home stood as a bastion of warmth against the winter's chill. Staff glided through corridors with efficient quietude, preparing for the day ahead. My mother, Nezhat, presided over the kitchen with a grace that belied the early hour. Her domain, a blend of Father's architectural elegance and the palpable warmth of familial love, buzzed softly with the promise of the day. The air was rich with the scents of brewing tea and warm cinnamon.

A sudden loud bang jolted her from her reverie. The door swung open abruptly as her youngest son banged into the doorframe, his momentum sending him into a quick pirouette before regaining his balance. I straightened, caught between excitement and the potential for being in trouble. Our eyes met; the world silent except for the ticking of the clock as Mother enveloped me in a hug. 'Sobh Bekheir (good morning), Shab jaan, you little terror,' she said, using the Farsi term of affection.

'Sobh Bekheir, Maman,' I replied with a politeness that quickly gave way to excitement. 'Have you seen outside? It's white. The whole world is white. It's snow, isn't it?'

Mother smiled, her eyes reflecting the soft light of the kitchen. 'Yes, my precious, it is snow. Dress for breakfast, and once you've eaten and its light, you can play outside.'

I clattered out of the kitchen and burst into the morning room, cheekily tapping the back of the newspaper Father was reading. 'Sobh Bekheir, Baba,' he greeted me.

'The world is white today,' I remarked, eyes wide with wonder.

'Indeed, it is, my son,' Father, Jalil, responded. 'A reminder of nature's beauty and its surprises.'

The breakfast spread before us was a testament to our family's prosperity and our cook's culinary prowess: traditional Iranian fare, including feta, walnuts, and dried fruit, wrapped in a soft taftoon flatbread intermixed with hints of our travels abroad, each dish a story of heritage and discovery. As we ate, the conversation ebbed and flowed like the tea in our cup.

I heard the muezzin at a nearby mosque reciting the Adhan, the dawn call to prayer. My family was not devout, and I usually tuned out the calls, but this morning the snow amplified the melodic and haunting tones of the Adhan being recited in Arabic.

Thirty minutes later, Father departed. He always left at 6.00 am to walk eight miles until he could take a taxi to his office near the Grand Bazaar. I somehow managed to wait another hour until sunrise. By then, I had been joined by my constant companion Saeed, who had just returned to Iran with his parents from a spell living in Japan. We had an easy camaraderie, the divergence in our experiences contributing to a constant exchange of ideas.

Bundled up in warm coats and woollen mittens, we stepped outside. The crisp air bit at our cheeks, the scent of burning wood from nearby homes mingling with the fresh cleanliness of snow. We were met by the sight of two men shovelling snow, their breaths visible in the chill morning air. 'We're here to clear your drive or balcony,' they announced, their voices echoing in the quiet of the snowy dawn.

In the extensive gardens of our family home, Saeed and I found ourselves in a wonderland of glistening snow. The early morning had draped a soft blanket over every hedge and path, transforming familiar landscapes into scenes from a fairy tale. With the brightness of the winter sun casting long, playful shadows across the snow, our laughter echoed through the crisp air.

With a mischievous glint in his eye, I scooped up a handful of snow, compacting it with eager hands that trembled slightly from excitement. I aimed and threw the snowball with a triumphant yell, watching as it arced through the air, landing with a soft thud against Saeed's shoulder.

Saeed, momentarily surprised, stared at the snow dusting his coat before his face split into a wide, challenging grin. The game was on. We darted around the garden, with each throw and dodge bringing a burst of exhilaration.

As we played, the garden became a maze of trails and laughter, each corner a new chapter of the adventure as we built a snowman, placing a carrot for the nose and using stones for the eyes.

We broke for lunch at 1.30 pm when a huge sparkling green and chrome Pontiac turned into the long drive and rolled to a stop near the house. Father climbed out first. He came home at this time every day for lunch and a siesta, and then worked in his study until the evening.

Usually my uncle Ahad, three years younger than Father, drove them and stayed for lunch, after which they sat discussing politics.

When the siestas started, I quietly wandered off and found Saeed again to resume the fun. But it was not just play; it was a sharing of spirits and dreams. As we paused, panting and laughing under the bare branches of an old oak, I spoke of the school we would soon attend and Saeed of the games we would play, our voices earnest and full of hope.

By the time the afternoon sun began to claim the snow, turning the pristine white into glistening patches of wet ground, we were tired but content, lying on our backs and watching as the clouds drifted lazily across the winter sky, the cold seeping through our coats.

As we finally trudged back towards the house, leaving a trail of muddy footprints on the snow's edge, the garden bore the marks of our day; a testament to the joy and unbridled freedom that a winter's day offered to the hearts of the young. In years to come, this day, like the garden, would remain a cherished memory, a symbol of the simplicity and beauty of childhood friendship. How could I possibly have known what was to come?

FROM TABRIZ TO TEHRAN

Father had long before discovered that the world is far from all white. Born in the serene province of Tabriz, bordering Russia in north-western Iran, his early years had been marked by the comforts of an affluent life; his childhood estate dominated by a large swimming pool big enough to row a boat across, a testament to his family's wealth and status. Parked in the drive was the first American car in the town, a symbol of modern luxury and his father's pioneering spirit in business, accumulating assets including cinemas, a leather factory, dried fruit export business, farms and other properties.

Tabriz was home to the beautifully rebuilt fifteenth-century Blue Mosque, retaining the original turquoise mosaics on its entrance arch, and the Middle East's largest covered bazaar, a sprawling brick-vaulted complex selling carpets, spices and jewellery. Yet, the tranquillity of this idyllic setting was disrupted during the Second World War when Russian forces occupied Iranian Azerbaijan, to secure a supply route to the Soviet Union and counter potential German influence in the region. Their occupation lasted until 1946, despite promises of rapid withdrawal after the war. They also helped themselves to most business assets and those of Father's family were no exception.

At the beginning of the invasion, the Russians commandeered the Hashtroudi residence for its grandeur and strategic location, converting the family's sanctuary into a military headquarters. Young Jalil was among those captured and was thrown down the stairs by an angry soldier, an act that left a lasting scar on his abdomen – a constant reminder of the occupation and an unkind novelty for the family. 'Jalil, you must understand, these are turbulent times,' his father would explain, his voice a mixture of frustration and resignation. They sat in the dim light of the study, the once vibrant walls now dulled by the shadow of military presence. 'We must endure and adapt. Our home is no longer ours alone.'

Jalil was excelling not only in his academic studies, but also on the football field. This had brought unexpected benefits. His prowess as a footballer for the Tabriz national team drew crowds, among them Nezhat, a young woman from a neighbouring town. She was captivated by his athletic grace and wet slicked-back hair, and sparked a romance that would define both their futures. 'Nezhat, have you seen the way he plays? He's not just running after a ball; he's like a poet in motion,' her friend whispered during one of the matches, as they watched Jalil skilfully navigate the field.

In the cool evening air of a community gathering, Jalil caught Nezhat's gaze across the crowded space, their mutual fascination palpable in the charged atmosphere. As they found themselves side by side, Jalil, with a smile that softened his usually stern demeanour, leaned in and whispered, 'Your passion for the game is as captivating as the game itself.' Nezhat, her dark eyes sparkling with amusement and intrigue, replied, 'And your prowess on the field is only matched by your eloquence off it.'

Their courtship blossomed with each encounter, a blend of spirited debates and shared dreams under the vast, starlit skies of Tabriz. One evening, as they walked through the quiet streets, Jalil shared his aspirations with a tone of earnest conviction. 'Nezhat, imagine us in Tehran, where the future is being built every day. There's a vibrancy there that Tabriz, for all its beauty, can't match.' Captivated by his vision and deeply in love, Nezhat responded, her voice tinged with a mix of excitement and apprehension, 'It's a daunting step, Jalil. But if it's with you, I'm ready to embrace whatever this new city holds.'

Their move to Tehran was a leap into a bustling world far removed from Tabriz's provincial calm. The capital, with its relentless pace, was exhilarating yet alienating, a stark contrast to the familiar landscapes of their youth. As they navigated through

Tehran's sprawling urban maze, finding new favourites among its myriad bazaars and cafés, Jalil and Nezhat slowly wove their old habits with new routines. Over time, Tehran's cacophony turned into a symphony they cherished, echoing the adventurous spirit that had driven them from their home. Yet, in quieter moments, the echoes of Tabriz's serene mountains and the cold whispers of its winters would drift through their minds. Jalil, looking out over the balcony of their new home one evening, said softly, 'This city sings with opportunity, Nezhat, but the melodies of Tabriz – it's where our story began.'

FATHER, THE ENTREPRENEUR

Jalil and Ahad were finding their way around the vibrant city of Tehran, after moving from the tranquillity of Tabriz. They had just entered the city's Grand Bazaar, with its labyrinthine alleys teeming with traders and artisans. It was here, among the echoes of haggling voices and the rich smells of spices and leather that the brothers saw their chance.

'Look at this place, Ahad,' Jalil remarked, his eyes reflecting the vibrant life of the bazaar. 'Every corner, every stall is brimming with possibilities. It's like navigating a sea of opportunities, each wave bringing us closer to what we've dreamed of.'

Ahad, his gaze lingering on a craftsman expertly working leather, nodded thoughtfully. 'It's about harnessing the right opportunity, Jalil. Our heritage in Tabriz, our experience of leather – it's unique, and it's what Tehran needs.'

Jalil's smile broadened at the affirmation. 'Exactly! We're not just selling leather; we're offering a piece of our history, the art of our forebears. We'll blend tradition with Tehran's growing demand for quality and style.'

In the bustling heart of Tehran, they began to sketch the outlines of what would become a flourishing business. After much discussion, they secured a modest office space just a stone's throw from the Grand Bazaar. It was a small, unassuming room, but to them, it symbolised a beginning filled with promise. Jalil stood at the threshold of the new office, his eyes taking in the bare walls that would soon witness their entrepreneurial journey. 'This is it, Ahad. From here, we build not just a business and a future, but also a legacy. We start small, gain the trust of the shoemakers, and slowly expand. Our ties to the finest leather craftsmen in Tabriz will give us an edge.'

As they set up their workspace, Nezhat came by to see the place. She looked around the bare office and smiled. 'I can almost hear the buzz of success. You two are going to fill this place with life, just as you've planned.'

Jalil laughed: 'With your support and a bit of good fortune, this vision will indeed become a reality.'

The initial months were a test of their resilience. The brothers met with countless shoemakers, their pitches honed to emphasise the unmatched quality and heritage of their leather. 'This isn't just material; it's the essence of Tabriz, crafted into every piece,' Jalil would explain, his passion evident. Their breakthrough came when a well-known shoemaker, captivated by the quality of their leather, placed the first significant order. That evening, in a quaint café near their office, the brothers celebrated this milestone.

As their reputation grew, so did their operations. The small office no longer sufficed. They moved to a larger space, now with a view of the bustling streets that had once intimidated them. With every leather shipment, with every satisfied client, their confidence soared, establishing their foothold in Tehran's burgeoning market. Through perseverance and a keen understanding of quality, Jalil and Ahad rapidly grew their modest start-up into a vital part of Tehran's industrial landscape, laying a foundation that would support their families for years to come.

The business thrived and soon, Jalil and Ahad found themselves at a crossroads. The demand for their leather outstripped their initial forecasts, prompting a discussion on expansion. Jalil had already thought about this. Demand was strong and he thought customers would increase their orders if the business had more to sell at an acceptable price. However, there was a shortage of fine leather. Producers had used the situation to increase their prices and retailers were forced to absorb the extra cost to keep customers happy or increase prices to share the burden. Jalil was adamant. 'The market in Tehran needs more leather,' he said. 'If we can be the company to supply it, we can get back to the old prices and make more sales.'

Jalil knew where to look, both inside and outside Iran. He began telephoning importers, while Ahad started probing remote areas and other provinces. If they could go straight to the producers, they could cut out the middleman, reducing costs while increasing the supply.

This new purchasing strategy proved to be a great success. They found that the simple act of visiting their suppliers with small gifts helped them to build good relationships, thereby securing their supply chains.

At the same time, they became swamped in paperwork. There were piles of letters, offers, orders, delivery instructions and other documents on every horizontal surface. They again moved to a larger office and turned to Jalil's cousin, Samad, to run it. Samad was an experienced accountant who had worked for a major bank with rigid procedures for managing customer information and other records. He arranged detailed files in a large four drawer metal cabinet, almost as tall as he was, indexing everything for easy reference. 'It looks as if we have the most modern and well-organised office in the whole of Tehran,' said Ahad.

A few weeks later Jalil and Ahad expanded the payroll with another salesman to help find buyers. The business prospered, its growth mirroring the evolving landscape of Tehran itself – modern, ambitious and forward-looking. Everything was good. But they recognised that they were very dependent on one industry.

One late summer evening, as the brothers discussed future plans in Jalil's study amid the sounds of happy children splashing in the swimming pool in the background, Jalil proposed, 'Ahad, why don't we diversify and expand into something complementary? Leather is just the beginning.'

Ahad, intrigued, leaned forward. 'What do you have in mind?'

'Dried fruits and nuts,' Jalil responded, his voice tinged with excitement. 'Iran's pistachios, dates, and almonds are prized globally. Why not leverage our contacts to start exporting?'

Ahad nodded thoughtfully. 'It makes sense. It's a stable market and less affected by seasonal shifts unlike leather. Plus, it ties back to our roots in Tabriz, where agriculture thrives.'

Encouraged by Ahad's support, Jalil began contacting potential buyers overseas, leveraging the reputation they had built with leather to assure quality and reliability. 'Imagine,' Jalil said during a call with a distributor in Europe, 'providing your customers with the finest of Iran's produce, sourced with the same commitment to excellence as our leather.'

The response was overwhelmingly positive. Soon, orders began to flow not just for their leather but also for large shipments of dried fruits and nuts. The brothers set up a small processing unit near their office, where the raw produce was cleaned, sorted and packaged under strict quality control measures.

'Seeing our products ready for export gives me a sense of pride,' Ahad remarked one day as they inspected a batch of pistachios destined for Europe.

Jalil, standing beside a stack of neatly labelled boxes, shared his vision. 'This is just the beginning, Ahad. These boxes carry more than just produce; they carry a promise of quality and a piece of our homeland.'

As the venture grew, so did their reputation. Jalil and Ahad were soon regarded not just as successful businessmen but as pioneers who introduced Tehran's market dynamics to the world. Nezhat, ever supportive, marvelled at their progress. 'You two have truly turned a vision into reality,' she said during a celebration dinner.

The success in dried fruits and nuts not only broadened their business scope but also cushioned them against the volatility of the leather market. It was a testament to their foresight and adaptability, qualities that defined their journey from the alleys of Tabriz to the bustling economic corridors of Tehran.

The business flourished and provided good support for their families. They were each soon able to buy prime land and have renowned architects build them beautiful homes. The Hashtroudi mansion soon echoed with the joyful cries of children. Nadereh, the first-born, arrived on a crisp autumn morning in 1946. Her first steps were cautious yet determined, watched eagerly by her proud parents. 'Look at her go, Nezhat!' Jalil exclaimed with a broad smile, 'She's as determined as you.' Massoud followed in the summer of 1947, his first words charmingly mispronounced, eliciting laughter at every family gathering. 'It seems he'll be a talker, just like his father,' Nezhat noted. Hedayat, born in 1950, was the quiet observer, his curious eyes taking in every detail. When he finally decided to walk, he did so with a steadiness that surprised everyone. 'He's our little philosopher,' Jalil would say, watching Hedayat explore the garden's hidden nooks.

COUP D'ÉTAT

But trouble was brewing. In the heart of Tehran, under the shadow of the Alborz Mountains, the air carried whispers of change. It was 1953, the year before I was born. Indeed, I had already been conceived, but Mother was awaiting confirmation that she was with child. And it was a year that would be etched in the annals of Iran's history with the ink of turmoil and change. Jalil and Nezhat's home, usually a vibrant forum for lively debates fuelled by endless cups of tea and a few beers, had fallen under a veil of quiet contemplation. The once-passionate arguments about politics and current events had devolved into hushed conversations, laced with a newfound caution. The culprit? A political earthquake that had shaken Tehran to its core in the shape of Iran's coup d'état.

Jalil championed open dialogue. His study, overlooking the shimmering expanse of the swimming pool bathed in the warm glow of the setting sun, had often served as the stage for these intellectual jousts. Now, however, as he sat there reflecting on the recent events, a sense of unease gnawed at him. The overthrow of the democratically elected prime minister, Mohammad Mosaddegh, in favour of bolstering the shah's monarchical rule, exposed the precariousness of democracy. It laid bare the power struggles that simmered beneath the surface of national politics, entangled with the machinations of international forces.

The simmering tensions had their roots in the rise of nationalist sentiment. Mossadegh, a popular figure, had spearheaded the nationalisation of Iran's oil industry in 1951. This move challenged the decades-long control held by the Anglo-Iranian Oil Company, a British entity. The nationalisation ignited a period of intense societal participation in politics. Public demonstrations, like the July 1952 uprising, roared in support of Mossadegh's defiance.

However, from the perspective of Britain, Iranian oil had become a strategic lifeline, especially during World War II, explaining the Anglo-Soviet invasion of Iran in 1941. The Cold War further complicated the situation. The Soviets, vying for influence in northern Iran during 1945–46, sought oil concessions bordering their territory. Britain, determined to maintain control over this vital resource and the wealth it generated, saw the nationalisation as a direct threat. Mosaddegh's vision for a sovereign Iran had ignited the flames of nationalism but had also drawn the ire of powerful adversaries.

Understanding the complex web of interests that culminated in the coup only deepened Father's concern. The overthrow of a democratically elected leader cast a long shadow over the future of Iran, the name of which had been formally preferred by the government over the Greek Persia since 1935. He wondered what this meant for the country's political trajectory and the lives of his family, especially children, who were yet to understand the complexities of their heritage. How would the changes shape their identities, their dreams, and their sense of belonging in a nation caught between the glories of its ancient past and the uncertainties of its modern reality?

Father knew that the history he was living would one day serve as a guide for his grandchildren. It was his hope that, through understanding the struggles of their ancestors, they would find the strength to face their own challenges, to contribute to the rebuilding of a nation that stood proud in its rich heritage and hopeful in its future. He turned to his writing desk, surrounded by piles of notes and open books. The task of documenting the tumultuous times was not only a personal duty but a historical responsibility. He wrote not just for his heirs, but for all those who would seek to understand the soul of Iran, its trials and its resilience. He wrote of the days leading up to the coup, of the palpable tension in the air as rumours swirled through the streets of Tehran, whispers of foreign interference and internal betrayal.

As he wrote, his mind wandered back to the vibrant bazaars, the heartbeats of Tehran's social life, now subdued. The bazaars had always been more than just marketplaces; they were where culture thrived, where news travelled fastest and where the spirit of Iran was most alive. He remembered the lively debates over cups of chai, the laughter and the shared dreams of a brighter future. Now, uncertainty shadowed these gatherings, the joy replaced by cautious whispers, the openness by suspicion. Turning a page in his notebook, Jalil began to document the moment of Mosaddegh's arrest, an event that had shaken the foundation of Iranian democracy. He detailed the disbelief and despair that rippled through the community, the sense of betrayal that lingered in the air. This was not just the removal of a prime minister; it was an assault on the very ideals of sovereignty and self-determination that had inspired Iran's path towards modernity.

As the morning sun climbed higher, casting a warm glow over his desk, Father reflected on the role of intellectuals and educators like himself in navigating this new reality. They were the keepers of the flame, tasked with guiding the younger generation through the lessons of the past, equipping them with the knowledge and wisdom to rebuild and move forward. He wrote of his hopes for the future, for an Iran that would once again thrive on the principles of democracy and freedom and would stand proud on the world stage, not as a pawn in a greater geopolitical game, but as a testament to the indomitable will of its people. His last words on the page were a message of hope, a call to remember, to learn, and to strive for a better, more just Iran.

Father gathered his family in the living room, a modern space adorned with Persian carpets and heirlooms that told their own stories of Iran's rich history. The atmosphere was one of sombre anticipation as they all understood these moments together were not just for family bonding but for passing down wisdom and history that textbooks would never fully capture. He began to share his writings with them, his voice steady but filled with emotion as he recounted the events and their significance. His family listened intently, the younger ones with wide eyes, trying to grasp the complexities of a world that seemed far removed from the safety of their home. 'This is not just history,' he stressed, 'but a lesson on the cyclical nature of power, the importance of vigilance in safeguarding our rights, and the role each of us plays in the fabric of our nation.'

In the days that followed, Father's home remained a beacon of enlightenment and discussion, attracting friends, neighbours and colleagues who sought to understand and deliberate on the way forward for Iran. Inspired by Father's commitment to education and awareness, the younger generation in his family started to envision their roles in shaping a future where such coups would be relegated to the pages of history, never to be repeated. This legacy of intellectual curiosity and civic responsibility was a torch passed down, ready to be carried forward by those who had not yet come into the world but whose path would be illuminated by the wisdom of their forebears.

Tehran Grand Bazaar

CHAPTER SEVEN:
THE LIGHT OF THE HOUSE

By all accounts, my arrival in 1954 brought a burst of energy into the household. My first laugh was loud and infectious, setting off a chain reaction of giggles among my siblings. 'He will be the light of this house,' Father declared, holding me close during a family dinner.

Lastly, Shahin entered the world in 1960, his first word – 'ball' – foretelling his future passion for sports. 'Another athlete, perhaps?' Father mused to Mother as they watched Shahin crawl determinedly towards a football.

Such moments, small yet profoundly significant, were the threads that wove the fabric of the Hashtroudi family's life in Tehran, each child adding more character to the family.

Throughout the 1950s and 60s, Iran underwent significant economic and social changes, spurred by an oil revenue boom and modernisation efforts. Tehran became a bustling metropolis, a melting pot of new ideas and technologies that reshaped everyday life. Father and Mother watched as their children grew up in a world far different from their own childhoods. 'It's amazing, isn't it?' Father remarked one evening, turning the dial on their newly acquired television, a symbol of modern luxury. 'To think that our children will see the world not just through stories but through this screen.' Mother, arranging a tray of snacks brought back from their latest trip to a European-inspired supermarket, nodded. 'And they're learning English so young. It's the language of the world now, isn't it? Our Tehran is no longer just ours. It's part of something much bigger.'

The streets around them hummed with the new cars and cinemas that now showed foreign films were regular outings for the family. Us children adapted swiftly, blending Persian traditions with the Western customs that were now in vogue. 'This city, it's changing every day,' Jalil observed as Ahad drove his sparkling green and chrome Pontiac through the newly constructed highways that cut across the city. 'And we must change with it. It's the only way to ensure our children have a place in this new Iran.'

As the city grew, the family's social circle expanded to include expatriates and diplomats, introducing them to even more diverse cultures and cuisines. Dinner parties at the Hashtroudi residence often featured discussions on global politics and economics, reflecting Tehran's increasingly international character. And, as Tehran grew, so did our aspirations. Father and Mother embraced the changes, seeing them as avenues to educate their children about the world beyond Iran's borders, preparing them for the global stage they would one day step onto. For them, education was not just a formality but a vital bridge to the world beyond Iran's borders. They instilled in their children the belief that learning was the gateway to opportunity and personal growth. 'Education is your passport, my dears,' Jalil would often say at the dinner table, his eyes sweeping across the faces of his children. 'And a well-stamped passport at that, opening doors in corners of the world you've yet to imagine.'

Nezhat, always supportive of her husband's visions, added, 'We want you all to have the best, to be the best. That's why your schools are not just any schools. They are the best Tehran offers.' The children, each at different stages of their academic journey, felt the weight and the promise of these expectations. For Nadereh, Massoud and Hedayat, this meant excelling in their Tehran schools was just the beginning. The true test would come abroad, in the United Kingdom, where they were sent to further their studies in a more competitive and diverse educational environment.

THE GRAND RESIDENCE

Commanding a prominent position on a rise in the vibrant Shemiran district of Tehran, a stone's throw from the shah's opulent palace, the Hashtroudi residence reigned supreme. A monument to Father's achievements and love for modern design, it wasn't merely a house; it was a symphony of light and space, meticulously crafted by a renowned American architect. Born under its watchful gaze, the residence would become an indelible part of my life. The façade of the house was a marvel of geometric precision, with clean lines and expansive windows that allowed light to cascade into the spacious interiors. The meticulously chosen materials spoke volumes. The local stone, buffed to a soft sheen, shimmered under the Tehran sun, while inside, cool Italian marble throughout offered a luxurious respite from the summer's relentless heat.

Through the grand gates of the Hashtroudi estate, an air of grandeur and spaciousness settled over every visitor. A porte-cochère large enough to house a fleet of a dozen gleaming Mercedes or Cadillacs marked the entrance, while meticulously maintained gardens, bursting with colourful blooms and fragranced with jasmine, disappeared into the distance, dotted with statues and sparkling fountains. The imposing modern-day mansion, a testament to Jalil Hashtroudi's success, stood at the end, completing the scene. The grand entrance hall, its polished marble floor reflecting the light from a striking chandelier, boasted high, vaulted ceilings. Minimalist décor emphasised the expansive space, designed for entertaining on a grand scale – perhaps lavish dinner parties or soirées filled with music.

Beyond this impressive entryway, the house flowed into a series of fluid living spaces, prioritising not just beauty, but the comfort of its inhabitants. One such space was Father's study. Book-lined walls surrounded a large, ornately carved desk, while a comfortable sitting area with plush armchairs invited discussion. Glass doors provided a seamless connection to the sun-drenched swimming pool and landscaped gardens. As I was growing up, these outdoor spaces became my summer playground. Tehran's heat seemed relentless, but the pool offered a cool escape. My siblings and I would spend hours splashing, our laughter echoing off the house. By summer's end, my skin would be bronzed to a deep hue, earning me the playful nickname Seeah – Blacky – from Mother.

The garden was a symphony of colours and scents. Fragrant jasmine mingled with the sweet perfume of roses, while towering cypresses cast long shadows on winding pathways that beckoned further exploration. There were twenty cherry trees along the driveway; in spring, the blossom was magical. There was a greenhouse overflowing with lush greenery, tended by the full-time gardener, Mash Hedayat, who was in his late sixties, but strong and hard working. A wild patch, a haven for urban wildlife, thrived next door, its gnarled trees and overgrown bushes a stark contrast to the manicured gardens. Here, I observed sparrows, pigeons, migrating birds and even a shy hedgehog. On the edge of this valiant little wildlife preserve were some fascinating examples of pond life. Finally, the pièce de résistance was a beautiful walled kitchen garden. Basking in the sun, it became a less inviting retreat during the hottest days, but in milder weather, it was a haven for lethargic buzzing insects and a source of endless fascination for me.

Mother taught me about herbs and their amazing range of textures, from the feathery fronds of dill to the rough, fuzzy leaves of sage, and how each unique aroma and flavour could elevate a simple dish. She'd also point out the vibrant, fragrant flowers, some specifically chosen to adorn the house with their beauty, and others, like the pansies, with petals delicate enough to be sprinkled across a salad. I couldn't help but smile when I would hear Mother, during grand soirées, regale guests with tales of her 'secret weapon' of goat cheese adorned with nasturtium blossoms, borage flowers and pansy petals, or a simple green salad brought alive with a scattering of pastel-coloured violas.

Back inside, the upper floor offered a haven from the summer heat. The six bedrooms and bathrooms alongside a casual family space were impressive, but it was the wraparound balcony that truly held magic. Here, the family could mitigate the blistering summer heat at night. Cool night air washed over them like a balm as they sprawled on comfortable divans, their gazes fixed on the breathtaking expanse above. Unlike most cityscapes, Tehran's night sky remained untainted by light pollution, a vast tableau of twinkling stars. These quiet moments on the balcony were sacred to us. Stories whispered under the celestial kaleidoscope and dreams woven in the cool night air became treasured memories. I would stay awake for hours, mesmerised by the ever-shifting galaxy above and feeling close enough to touch the stars.

As I grew older, the house remained a constant in my life, a symbol of stability and love. The lessons learned within its walls, from the value of hard work to the importance of family, shaped me into the man I would become. It was more than a house; a home built on the foundation of my parents' aspirations and filled with hopes for the future. Mornings were lively and filled with routine, beginning with the aromatic waft of coffee and fresh Barbari bread from the kitchen. Mother, up before anyone else, orchestrated the morning's activities with a conductor's precision. The kitchen, spacious and well appointed with modern appliances juxtaposed against traditional Iranian décor, was her realm. Here, she prepared not just meals but also produced packed lunches for us to take to school.

Breakfast was a communal affair, a time when the family gathered at the large table laden with a spread of cheeses, fresh fruits, nuts and honey, often punctuated by Father reading from the morning paper. Afternoons brought us back home, our voices filling the house with stories from their day at school. Mother would often be found in the garden, tending to her flowers or sitting under the shade of a tree to hear her children recount their day. This ritual was a cherished part of daily life. As evening settled, the family would often dine outside under the stars during the warmer months, the garden providing a perfect backdrop for evening meals. Then, Father would retreat to his study, a sanctuary of historical artefacts, lined with shelves that reached the ceiling, filled with literature on philosophy, history, politics and economics. The large desk at the centre of the room, cluttered with papers and antique writing instruments, was where he penned letters, drafted plans and made decisions that would impact not just his family but also his growing business empire.

The grand residence was more than just a home; it was a sanctuary where each family member's unique interests and affections were nurtured under one roof. The daily routines, from lively breakfast discussions to the tranquil afternoons in the garden, were threads woven into the fabric of their collective life, binding them with a sense of unity and belonging. As night fell and the dinner conversations faded into the soft shadows of the evening, the house would quiet down, each corner echoing the laughter and debates of the day.

WEEKENDS WITH THE FAMILY

The excitement was palpable in the grand Hashtroudi residence. The working week in Iran stretches from Saturday to Thursday, following the rhythms set by the Muslim faith where Fridays serve as a day of rest and communal prayer. The school week was only five-and-a-half days, as was Father's work schedule. Accordingly, the family would gather at home on a Thursday afternoon to wind down and prepare an enjoyable and leisurely weekend. As dusk fell on Thursday evenings, Tehran's cafés and restaurants hummed with life, their lights casting a warm glow against the cool evening air. Families, freed from the confines of their weekday routines, ventured out into the night. In popular areas, the pavements would overflow with couples and families all clearly destined for the city's culinary and cultural delights, while the curbs filled nose to tail with parked cars of the era.

I was fascinated by grand vehicles. On one outing I spotted both an American Cadillac Eldorado Seville, a massive two-door hardtop coupe with a distinctive wraparound windscreen and tailfins, and a German Mercedes-Benz Gullwing with doors that swung up vertically over the roof making it look as if the car might fly away. I loved these outings. The family would often start early with a visit to an ice cream parlour or sometimes begin at our favourite restaurant, a place where the aroma of rich stews and grilled meats filled the air, mingling with laughter and music.

With youthful enthusiasm, I would watch spellbound as kebabs sizzled over open flames and rice steamed in large pots, each meal a culinary journey through the rich flavours of their heritage. The conversations at these gatherings were lively, punctuated with laughter and the animated storytelling of Father, who recounted tales of his youth with a zest that captivated his audience. Mother, always elegant, would add her insights and wisdom. These evenings were not merely about food; they were about nurturing the familial bonds that held us close.

After dinner, the family's journey would perhaps continue to one of Tehran's cinemas. Whether they stepped into the grandeur of a regular cinema or the novelty of an open-air screening, depending on the weather, each visit was an adventure. The silver screen brought tales from faraway lands, stories that sparked dreams and conversations. Wide-eyed and imaginative, I would immerse myself in the narratives, each film adding a layer to my understanding of the world. On special evenings, the family ventured to Café Nadery, a cornerstone of Tehran's social scene since the 1950s. Renowned for its intellectual gatherings, the café was a hub where poets, thinkers, and revolutionaries mingled, discussing ideas that could gently shift the societal sands.

For us, a visit to Café Nadery was like stepping into a living history book, each corner whispering secrets of the past. The café's atmosphere was electrifying, with the aroma of freshly brewed coffee blending with the scent of tobacco from old pipes, creating a heady mixture that seemed to stimulate conversation. The walls, lined with black-and-white photographs of illustrious patrons, echoed the cultural richness of the city. It was here, amidst debates and philosophical musings, that I began to form my own ideas about the world, inspired by the animated expressions of the café's patrons.

The allure of the cinema was a significant aspect of my childhood, particularly memorable on weekend nights. The anticipation would build throughout the day as my siblings and I speculated about the film we would see. Our father often chose the cinema as a treat after dinner, selecting from the array of theatres that dotted Tehran, each offering a window into different worlds through the flickering silver screen. Regular cinemas, with their grandiose interiors and plush seats, were a luxury, but the open-air cinema held a special charm, especially during the milder nights. Here, families gathered in their cars, the windows rolled down to welcome the cool evening breeze, as films projected on massive outdoor screens.

This was a communal experience, where the laughter and

applause rippled around the open space creating a collective joy that was rare and cherished. The films themselves were a mix of Hollywood blockbusters and Iranian cinema, reflecting the cultural duality that characterised Tehran in the 1960s. Imported films such as *Ben Hur* and *Lawrence of Arabia* captivated me with their epic stories and grand visuals, while Iranian movies offered narratives deeply rooted in Persian culture and history, providing a sense of pride and identity.

One of my enduring memories is attending an open-air cinema where the stage below the screen was a sea of geraniums. Local boys, who looked as if they couldn't afford the entry fee, were quietly climbing lampposts or perching on nearby walls to catch a glimpse of the big screen. These cinema outings were not just entertainment; they were cultural lessons, discussion starters, and a foundation for dreaming. After each movie, the drive home would be filled with discussions about the storylines and characters, debates over the best scenes, and sometimes contemplative silence as they each lost themselves in the possibilities of the worlds they had just witnessed. For us, these cinema nights were more than just leisure; they were a bonding experience that nurtured our imaginations, expanded our understanding of the world, and enriched our weekend traditions.

Another weekend prime event was a visit to Ladan Ice Cream & Juice, an establishment that had woven itself into the fabric of local tradition, so much so that it was still trading when I checked more than fifty years later. The air inside the parlour was thick with the scent of fresh fruits and nuts, ingredients that were the cornerstone of their ice cream recipes. Here, the simple pleasure of a cold treat was elevated to an art form, with flavours that sang of both innovation and nostalgia. The Shahin ice cream parlour was also popular with the family, mainly for the passionate dedication of the owner, who manned the counter alone. Father, moved by the owner's commitment and the quieter ambience, often chose this spot for a more personal treat, supporting the underdog entrepreneur whose craft was his livelihood. It offered a reminder of the community's tight-knit fabric, where even an ice cream shop could serve as a pillar of support and friendship.

The weekend ritual was not just about indulgence but also about preparation for the social etiquette that threaded through Iranian culture. Taking cakes to a host's home was more than a courtesy: it was a symbol of respect and appreciation. Accordingly, the last stop on a weekend outing might be to a local bakery known as a haven for cakes and pastries. These excursions were not merely about satisfying a sweet tooth but were deeply woven into the culture of Tehran's social life. The act of sharing these treats with others was a gesture laden with meaning, reinforcing bonds and building bridges within the community. It was a practice that taught me the value of generosity and the joy of simple pleasures shared with loved ones. As the night deepened and their collection of desserts safely stowed, the family would return home, ready to distribute their bounty among friends and family. This tradition of dessert-sharing became a foundational memory for me, encapsulating the warmth and generosity so central to my upbringing.

NOWRUZ

Persian New Year celebration, known as Nowruz

Tehran experiences four seasons, with cold winters and exhaustingly hot summers. In the warmth of early spring each year, the Hashtroudi family, along with most households in Iran, prepared for the ancient festival that heralds the vernal equinox and embodies the spirit of renewal – Nowruz, the Persian New Year. 'This is not just a new year: it's a rebirth of everything we hold dear,' Father told me as we arranged Haft-Seen, the traditional table setting that includes seven items starting with the letter 'S' in the Farsi language. Each item symbolically represents essential life elements like love, health, and prosperity. Wide-eyed and curious, I watched as Father placed sabzeh, sprouted wheat grass, for rebirth and renewal, and samanu, a sweet pudding, for affluence and fertility.

'Why do we do this every year, Baba?' I asked, his fingers tracing the intricate patterns of the painted eggs, symbolising fertility.

'It's our heritage,' Father responded. 'Nowruz connects us to our ancestors, who observed the exact moment of the equinox to celebrate the triumph of light over darkness.' The room was filled with the fragrant scent of hyacinths and the sharp tang of vinegar, each item on the Haft-Seen part of the cultural identity. Outside, the streets of Tehran were alive with colour and sound. Families and friends visited one another, exchanging pastries and jumping over bonfires to cast off the year's misfortunes in a ritual called Chaharshanbe Suri (Wednesday Feast), which takes place on the eve of the last Wednesday of the year.

'Come, let's go see the bonfires,' Father said, leading me by the hand. As we stepped out, the crackling fires would light up their faces, and I would feel the warmth, not just from the flames but also from the community spirit around us. People of all ages laughed and sang, their voices rising into the night sky. 'This, Shab, is the heart of Nowruz – joy, community, and the warmth of family,' Father would explain, his eyes reflecting the firelight. 'We celebrate not just the new year but what we've survived and hope for what's to come.'

The arrival of Nowruz provoked a whirlwind of festive preparations; in the morning, Father, ever the stalwart of tradition, would lead the charge, ensuring that every corner of the house reflected the spirit of renewal that Nowruz embodies. 'Shab, it's time for khooneh tekouni, to shake the house clean,' he would declare, his voice echoing through the corridors. The phrase piqued my interest as I watched family and servants alike delve into the annual deep cleaning, scrubbing, sweeping, and polishing every surface.

'Why do we clean so thoroughly, Baba?' I asked.

'We cleanse our home to clear away the old year's dust and troubles, making room for good fortune to enter,' Father explained. 'It's not just our home we're renewing, but our hearts and minds too.'

Shopping for clothes added another layer of excitement. We visited crowded bazaars, where the air was thick with the aroma of spices and the clamour of merchants. We would buy 'new clothes for a new beginning to wear when we visit family and friends.'

'Each Nowruz is a chapter we write anew,' Jalil tells Shab as they stand before the completed Haft-Seen.

'And this year, we'll make it a beautiful one.' Father took great pride in teaching his children about the roots of Nowruz, which date back more than 3,000 years, intertwining with the history of the Zoroastrian religion, once predominant across Persia.

'Nowruz is not just a new year,' he would say. 'It's a message from our ancestors. It's about the triumph of light over darkness, warmth over cold, life over decay.' In our spacious living room, he would lay out old texts and scrolls, pointing to ancient symbols and scripts that detailed Nowruz rituals. 'Every element of Nowruz has its symbolism deeply rooted in our history,' he explained. We listened intently, absorbing the tales of kings and commoners who celebrated Nowruz as a time of hope and equity. As twilight merged into the soft glow of evening, Father would guide his family through the stories of bonfires that lit up the hillsides, symbolising the guiding light for the spirits of the dead, and the mirrors placed on tables reflecting the past and showing the future.

'These traditions connect us not only to our land but also to each other, across time and space,' he would say. I soaked in these lessons, understanding that Nowruz was more than just a cultural obligation; it was a celebration of the persistence of life, a festive affirmation of their heritage that stitched the fabric of their community together year after year. 'In this fast-moving world,' Father said, 'keeping our traditions alive is more crucial than ever. It keeps us grounded, reminds us of who we are and where we come from.'

During the festivities, Father's approach to his household staff was exemplary of his respect and care. He made it a point to ensure that the festivities were inclusive, extending the joyous atmosphere to every corner of their large household. Most of the servants, cooks, and gardeners were young adults who moved from outlying villages to Tehran for a better life.

My father always encouraged them to study and he would pay for their education at a nearby evening school. Most of them would stay with us for years and then go back to their villages to marry and settle down. 'Today, we are all family,' he would announce every year as he gathered everyone in the main hall, decorated with traditional Persian floral designs and the fragrant scent of jasmine. 'Nowruz is about renewal, and each of you is integral to the spirit of our home. Let's celebrate this new beginning together.'

One year, Father brought home a briefcase, from which he unveiled an exquisite collection of jewels and watches worth more than you could imagine. Each glittering treasure was mounted in its own ornate box, shimmering under the intense light from the chandeliers. The room hushed momentarily as all eyes turned to the gems before them. 'Pick one, each of you,' he announced, gesturing towards the open box with a warm smile. His eyes twinkled with a mischievous glint, knowing well the delight these gifts would bring. We eagerly leaned forward, our young faces alight with excitement as we chose a watch with the solemnity of knights selecting armour. As each family members took their turn, with jewellery for Mother and my sister and watches for the boys, Father called over the servants.

'Mohamad, you and your brother Ali Akbar have been with me since you were just boys. You must both have one each as well.' Mohamad, the elder, chose first, his fingers hesitating over the collection before selecting a watch with a deep blue face. Ali Akbar, returning later from the market, found himself drawn to the same style his brother had picked. The dispute that unfolded was swift and heated. Voices rose slightly above the usual festive buzz, drawing curious glances from the rest of the family. The argument reached its peak when, in a fit of anger, Ali Akbar smashed his chosen watch against the stone mortar and pestle from the kitchen, the beautiful timepiece shattering beyond recognition. The room fell silent, the joyous atmosphere dimmed by the sudden outburst.

Father's response was stern yet measured. He confiscated Mohamad's gift, much to the dismay of both brothers, leaving them watchless and remorseful. The festivity paused, a cloud of disappointment lingering over the gathering. However, Father couldn't bear the sombre turn of events for long. Days later, he returned from the bazaar with two identical watches, one for each brother, restoring not only peace but also reinforcing a powerful lesson about forgiveness and family unity.

'It is in these moments that we build not just a legacy of wealth but of character and respect,' he said. 'How we treat each other reflects the values we hold dear.' The incident became a testament to Father's wise and fair handling of conflicts, a story remembered and recounted with laughter and a hint of pride through three generations. It was these moments, filled with simple human emotions and resolutions, that truly defined the spirit of Nowruz in the Hashtroudi home – renewal not just of time but of bonds and understanding among those who shared their lives under one roof. As Nowruz concluded each year, the lessons of unity, respect, and compassion lingered, deeply ingrained in my young mind. These celebrations were not just about marking a new year; they reflected Father's commitment to fostering an environment where every individual felt honoured and included.

INTO THE MOUNTAINS

The majestic Alborz mountains stood as silent sentinels, guardians of history and the untamed wilderness beyond the urban sprawl of Tehran. They were an imposing backdrop to my daily playgrounds and one of my favoured weekend haunts: a place where the rigour of urban life gave way to the boundless freedom of nature. I cherished our mountain excursions. The journey from our home to the foot of the Alborz was a ritual in itself. Pedalling vigorously along winding paths with friends, we would escape the city's clamour. The transition was palpable: the air grew crisper, the sounds of traffic faded, and the city's skyline shrank behind us. By the time we dismounted our bicycles, the serene silence of the mountain was all-encompassing, save for the cheerful chatter of my companions.

Our destination was always the same – a secluded valley nestled between two peaks. Here, a small stream meandered through, its waters clear and cold, rushing over smooth stones and pebbles. It was an idyllic setting for the serious task at hand: studying for their impending exams. The tranquillity of the valley, with its lush greenery and the soft murmur of the stream, provided a perfect contrast to the usual study rooms' stifling air. We would spread our books under the generous shade of the trees, the soft rustle of leaves above mingling with the pages' flutter.

'This place, it's more than just our study spot, isn't it?' I remarked one afternoon, my voice low, almost blending into the surroundings.

'It's our sanctuary,' replied Saeed, looking around with a smile. 'Out here, it's like the world stands still, just for us.'

This natural haven did more than just soothe; it inspired. The purity of the surroundings, the sharpness of the air, and the gentle sounds of water were not just pleasant background but active participants in their process of learning. Discussions about mathematical formulas or historical dates were interspersed with pauses to appreciate a particularly melodious bird song or the sudden appearance of a mountain goat on a distant ridge. These moments, when nature intruded so gently into their studies, were reminders of the world's vastness and the small, perfect place they occupied within it.

'Imagine, all of history beneath these trees,' I mused, my hand gesturing towards the dense canopy. 'Generations have come and gone, but these mountains, they remain unyielding, witnessing our small triumphs and struggles alike.'

Each session by the stream deepened their connection to the land and to each other. It was here, amidst the discussions and discoveries, that I felt most acutely the passage of time – not just the hours of their study but the ebb and flow of seasons. The valley bore witness to their intellectual growth and their burgeoning friendships, rooted in shared experiences and mutual respect forged in the isolation of their mountain retreat.

As the exams approached, the urgency of their studies intensified, but so did our appreciation for their unique study hall. We knew that these days of freedom and learning were fleeting, as transient as the seasons themselves. Yet, this impermanence only added to the valley's charm, impressing upon them the importance of savouring each moment, each lesson learned not just from books but from the embrace of nature around them.

Their treks back home were reflective, the sunset casting long shadows as we retraced our steps, the mountains silhouetted against the sky. We left the valley each day with more knowledge and a greater sense of peace, carrying with us the profound tranquillity that only nature can bestow – a tranquillity that would fortify us for the challenges ahead.

'Each day we leave here richer than when we arrived,' I declared one evening, my eyes tracing the fading light over the peaks. 'And it's not just what's in our books. It's what's in our heads.'

Saeed nodded, his gaze lingering on the horizon. 'Yes, and whatever the future holds, we'll carry a piece of this place with us. Always.'

FLYING KITES

Crafting and flying of kites stood out as a particularly colourful pastime. The adventure began in the busy lanes near my home where the local dry cleaner supplied the necessary stiff brown paper, their rolls standing like sentinels amidst the steam and press of clothes.

The next step was the cobbler, a craftsman confined to a shop barely larger than a cupboard, who provided a special glue named sirish needed for kites. Potent and pungent, the glue was the secret to our kites' resilience in the robust spring breezes.

Hedi was the master kite maker. His hands, skilled from years of watching older artisans, moved with precision and grace. The final component was bamboo, essential for the kite's frame. This was 'borrowed' from the blinds in their servant's quarters, much to their father's chagrin.

'Hand me that bamboo strip, will you?' Hedi called out as he carefully aligned the pieces on their veranda, the spring air cool around them.

'Here you go,' I replied, passing the strip. I watched in awe as Hedi's fingers deftly tied the joints together. 'Do you think it'll fly as high as last year's?'

'Higher,' Hedi answered with a confident smile. 'With the right wind, it might just touch the clouds.'

Each kite was a labour of love, assembled with meticulous care, ensuring that each piece of bamboo fitted perfectly with the next, and that the paper was taut and flawless.

The kite flying itself was a ritual that summoned all the neighbourhood children. The skies above Tehran would blossom with kites, each a fluttering petal against the blue. My brothers and I would lead the charge, our kites soaring high, their tails whipping in the wind.

'The higher it flies, the better our year will be,' we shouted, eyes alight with excitement as we released our kites into the breeze.

Flying kites was more than just play: it was a dance of creativity and ingenuity, a challenge against the wind and a test of skill. Each successful launch was a triumph, each crash a lesson in persistence and resilience. The thrill of the kite's ascent, with the string tugging at one's fingertips, was a pure, exhilarating connection to the sky – a brief, glorious dominion over the air currents that swept across their city.

'These moments, they're what we'll remember when we're old and grey,' Hedi remarked, his gaze following a particularly daring kite dance above them.

'True,' I agreed, my voice filled with a mixture of joy and wistfulness. 'It's like holding a piece of the sky in our hands.'

One spring day, I discovered a hidden plot of empty land. It was just waiting to be occupied by the vivacious spirits of young dreamers. Ever the ringleader, I rallied my friends under the early morning sun and showed them how to climb the safer parts of the wall.

When we all stood in the long shadows gazing around the inside of the hidden enclosure that was soon to become our battleground of joy, I spoke in hushed tones. 'Look at this place. It's perfect for a football pitch!'

Saeed, always quick to catch on to my enthusiasm, jumped at the idea. 'But it's all overgrown, and those walls look ancient! How do we even start?'

'We start by making it ours,' I declared with a grin. 'We can flatten this land, set up goals, and it'll be our secret stadium.'

The boys, fuelled by youthful zeal and the thrill of a challenge, embarked on their project with gusto. They borrowed shovels and rakes, their days filled with the hard labour of clearing and levelling the ground. Each afternoon after school, we returned to our secret plot, our laughter and chatter a stark contrast to the quiet of the hidden land.

One day, as I was setting a makeshift goalpost, Father appeared unexpectedly. A moment of silence fell over us, the gravity of our trespass weighing down on them.

'What have you lads been up to?' his voice boomed, but his eyes twinkled with curiosity rather than anger.

Nervous yet honest, I stepped forward. 'We wanted a place to play, Baba. We meant no harm.'

Father surveyed the land, now markedly different from its former neglected state. 'You've done quite the job here,' he admitted, his tone softening. 'Let me talk to the owner. Maybe you can use it without having to sneak around.'

True to his word, Father negotiated with the landowner, who was impressed by our initiative and agreed to let us use the land officially. A few weeks later, a sturdy wooden gate replaced the portion of the wall we used to climb, signifying our rightful passage to the field.

Father, previously a professional footballer playing nationally for Tabriz, would sometimes show the family a few football tricks. One popular move saw him kick the ball high into the air so that it would come down and land in exactly the same place it had been previously. We thought that was so amazing.

One day, Father looked in to check all was well. One player called out, 'Mr Hashtroudi, please show us some of your trick shots.' At first, the former pro seemed reluctant, but eventually he relented and kicked the ball around for a while with skill and grace, much to everyone's delight. It was a wonderful little display and if nothing else it enhanced my standing as a footballer. Somehow, I gained reflected glory.

I often reminisced about the football matches on that pitch, the fierce games under the setting sun, where scores were settled by skill and sheer will. More than the games, it was the lessons of camaraderie, leadership, and community that stayed with me.

'Boys,' Father said, one evening as we walked home after a particularly exhilarating match, 'you've turned a forgotten patch into a field of dreams. Remember, it's not just about playing the game. It's about respecting your playmates, the ground you play on, and the community around you.'

These moments spent under the open sky were cherished episodes of freedom and happiness. These were times when the complexities of childhood gave way to simple pleasures, and when the skies above Tehran seemed vast and full of possibilities. For me and my brothers, each kite was not just a plaything but a vessel of dreams, each flight a testament to the boundless joy of our youthful days.

SUMMERS IN CHALLOUS

As Tehran's summer heat threatened to build to its oppressive crescendo each year, the Hashtroudi family would pack belongings. Over the years, our annual escape saw us squeeze into a sprawling burgundy and cream American Chevrolet, a white Rambler with a red interior and Uncle Ahad's chrome-finned Pontiac. With our patriarch at the wheel, we would embark on the northward journey to our summer haven on the Caspian Sea.

One of the world's natural marvels, the Caspian Sea claims a distinguished place, celebrated not only as the largest inland body of water but also as a crucial ecological and economic bastion. Nestled between the continents, this expansive sea is bordered by five countries, each drawing from its bountiful resources. Its significance extends beyond mere size; it is a critical habitat for a myriad of species, particularly the prized sturgeon, known for producing the coveted caviar.

The journey from Tehran to the serene Caspian shores is one of striking contrasts. Leaving behind the ceaseless rhythm of urban life, we travelled north, crossing diverse landscapes shifting from bustling cityscapes to tranquil rural settings, with a formidable trek through rugged mountains crowded with trucks and other large vehicles. It was an experience taking between six to eight hours and encompassing not only a physical transition but also a passage through the layers of Persian culture, where ancient traditions blend seamlessly with the echoes of modernity.

As Tehran fades in the rearview mirror, the air grows fresh, the skies widen, and the hustle of city life gives way to the soothing rhythms of the sea. The Caspian region, with its mild climate and lush surroundings, offers a respite from the arid conditions of the capital. Here, the coastlines are not just edges of land but gateways to peace, where the waters whisper tales of ages past and invite all who visit to pause and reflect on the enduring beauty of nature.

This majestic sea, often seen as a bridge between East and West, has fostered cultural exchanges and nurtured civilisations along its shores for millennia. It is a place where history is alive in the breeze, and every view tells a story of survival, adaptation, and co-existence. For residents of Tehran seeking escape or leisure, the Caspian Sea is a beloved destination, offering a blend of natural beauty and a reminder of the delicate balance that sustains life both in and around its waters.

Challous forms a beacon of tranquillity and natural splendour, tucked away along the northern coast, where the rugged beauty of the Alborz mountains provides a densely forested backdrop sweeping down to the gentle caress of the Caspian Sea. The sandy beaches come in stark contrast to Tehran's concrete jungle, offering expansive views that soothe the soul and mend the weariness of city life.

The coast here is dotted with fishing villages, quaint bungalows, cafés, and a few resorts like pearls strung along the shore, each offering a haven where time seems to slow, allowing for moments of reflection and connection with nature. Small-scale agriculture, particularly the cultivation of rice and citrus fruits, painted the surrounding low hills in vibrant shades of green and gold, and contributed to the local markets' abundance of fresh produce.

Culturally, Challous was a melting pot of its diverse inhabitants and their traditions. Local festivals, often marked by music, dance, and the sharing of food, highlight the calendar, drawing visitors into the communal heart of the region. These festivals are a vibrant expression of local identity and heritage, where ancient customs meet contemporary festivity.

On one of my first visits, everyone was amazed to discover that their patriarch had secretly commissioned a house to be built in honour of his wife. Planted gracefully on the sandy shores, our family's new beach home stood as a testament to Father's creativity and his devotion and profound love for his wife. He designed the house's front elevation to represent the letter 'N', a permanent homage to her name and a symbol of his affection.

I was inspired by the architect who designed the villa, a professional young Persian man who graduated as an architect in the USA. He was always smartly dressed, and he drove a convertible silver two-seater Mercedes, travelling to Challous from Tehran on a number of occasions for this project.

His architectural marvel blended modern design with traditional Persian elements. The façade was an intricate dance of geometry and grace, with broad, sweeping arches that invited the sea breeze into every corner of the home. The interiors were spacious and airy, designed to capture the essence of summer with their light, soothing colours and open-plan living spaces that seemed to extend seamlessly onto the beach.

The house served as the family's personal sanctuary, a place where the burdens of city life were washed away by the gentle murmurs of the Caspian waves. It was here that the Hashtroudis found their truest sense of togetherness, with each visit rekindling the bonds that the hectic pace of Tehran often left strained. The living room, with its large glass windows, offered panoramic views of the azure waters, turning every meal into a picturesque scene that looked to have come straight out of a painting.

Each room was thoughtfully appointed to ensure comfort while echoing the natural beauty outside. The children's bedrooms were decorated with motifs of sea and sand, fostering a love for nature and adventure in the young minds. My room faced the sea and I usually fell asleep to the sound of the waves, dreaming of the adventures the next day might bring.

Outside, the large garden was a lush oasis full of citrus trees, mainly oranges, that helped quench our summer thirst, with native flora that bloomed vibrantly throughout the summer months, allowing Mother to decorate the main rooms with the colours and fragrance she loved. A path of smooth stones, flanked by flowering shrubs and tall palms, led directly to the beach.

The property was expansive, stretching generously along the beachfront, where the golden sands met the gentle waves nuzzling the shore. The early mornings at Challous were particularly enchanting, as the early light danced on the water's surface, turning it into a shimmering display of blues and golds. As a young boy, I was captivated by this display, watching it from my bedroom window before running down to the water's edge and wading along to the hive of activity where the local fishermen, rugged and bronzed from years under the sun, were preparing for another arduous day.

Fishing was an ancient and critical part of the local economy. Traditional fishing boats, probably *telambārs* – large, broad, curving wooden hulls, open to the elements and rowed laboriously by a dozen oarsmen, with an enormous jumble of nets overflowing two-thirds of the deck space – would fight their way through the onshore surf to calmer waters beyond. These rugged craft were without sails, but some seemed to have unseen motors. Covering a wide loop about two to three miles, the men cast nets that would later enclose the bounty of the Caspian when they returned in the afternoon.

I would watch intently as the boats returned, slamming through the breakers to reach the shore where a crowd had gathered. The community came alive, everyone from young children to the elderly eager to see the catch. The nets, heavy and soaked, were hauled onto the beach, revealing their contents to the excited onlookers. Among the day's catch were numerous white fishes, flapping in the firm mud, but the stars of the show were the sturgeons – a rare sight that drew gasps from the crowd.

One day, there was a sturgeon, about a yard long and weighing-in at around twenty-five pounds, that was the focus of much attention. I observed as an experienced fisherman carefully slit the belly of the sturgeon, allowing a long strip of black caviar, the roe – its eggs – to tumble and slide into a pan. This delicacy, known for its rich flavour and high value, was treated with utmost care. Every last little egg was carefully scooped into pre-printed metal cans, the lids pressed on by hand with a pinch of salt added – a nod to the tastes of the American market.

My family would gather on our veranda in the evenings to watch the sunset painting the sky in strokes of orange and purple, dine on the day's catch and discuss the day's events. In the distance, we could hear the banter of fishermen as they maintained their nets, repairing damaged areas and laying them carefully so they would pay out smoothly without catching or tangling. I was astounded by the amount of hard labour required.

When I spoke of this, Father took the opportunity to explain in detail to his family the economic dynamics of the caviar trade. His voice carried the weight of experience and knowledge as he detailed how the fishing industry not only supported the local community but also connected their small town to global markets. A five-pound can of this caviar could fetch about $55 in Tehran and upwards of $200 in the US, a significant sum that illustrated the economic importance of these fish.

The discussions enriched the evenings, blending seamlessly with the sounds of the sea and the laughter of family gatherings. As night fell, the stories and lessons from the day mingled with the rhythmic lapping of the waves, embedding deep in my heart the values of hard work, respect for nature, and the intricate balance of local traditions and global interactions.

On one occasion, the drive from Tehran was abruptly overshadowed by a near-tragic incident. Emerging from a lengthy tunnel into a thick fog, a car ahead failed to navigate a sharp bend and plunged down the cliff. The accident prompted an immediate response from Father and other drivers. They quickly formed a human chain, meticulously stretching down the steep embankment. Brave younger volunteers descended to the wreckage where they found a family trapped inside. With concerted effort, they extracted the father, his friend, and his son from the mangled vehicle just as emergency services arrived. Miraculously, the family suffered only minor injuries.

On that day, the rest of the drive to the villa was subdued, the events of the incident casting a long shadow over the family. Upon arrival, the exhaustion of the ordeal was palpable. Father, overwhelmed and fatigued by the day's emotions and activities, fell asleep on the sofa, a testament to the day's strain. The incident left an indelible mark on me, highlighting the road's inherent dangers and the resilience and quick thinking of the rescuers. It was a day of sharp contrasts: the perilous beauty of our journey, sudden descent into chaos, and the communal spirit that brought them back to safety.

'How does everyone just … come together like that in moments of real danger?' I mused.

Father had a thoughtful expression. 'It's about community,' he said. 'In times of crisis, differences fade into the background. What emerges is our innate need to help, to connect, to protect one another. It's a powerful reminder of our shared humanity.'

The distant sounds of the sea provided a soothing backdrop as I digested Father's words. 'It's like each person's effort weaves into a larger safety net,' I mused, looking out towards the darkened waves.

'Yes, exactly,' Father nodded, pleased with this understanding. 'And it's these experiences that shape us, that teach us about courage, about the importance of being there for each other. These lessons are as crucial as any knowledge you might gain from books or school.'

They sat in silence for a moment, each lost in their thoughts, the rhythmic sound of the waves punctuating the quiet. I felt a renewed sense of connection to the world around me, emboldened by the day's events and Father's insights.

As we rose to head back inside, Father placed a reassuring hand on my shoulder. 'Remember this day, Shab. Remember the strength found in unity. It's a meaningful lesson that will guide you well, no matter where your journey takes you.'

It was a perfect end to a day that had seen both the best and worst of what life could offer, a reminder of the delicate balance we all navigate.

CHAPTER EIGHT:
BLACK GOLD

Barely ten but with a curiosity as vast as the sea, I sat cross-legged on the ornate Persian carpet in Father's study, as Father began one of his fascinating tales. 'Shab,' he began, his voice a blend of enthusiasm and solemnity, 'our land is steeped in black gold, as old as the legends of the fire worshippers.' He gestured expansively, as if unveiling an invisible map. 'For thousands of years, from the time of the great Darius, our ancestors used the oil seeping from the ground. They used it for medicine, to light their lamps, and to seal their boats.'

My eyes widened with wonder, my mind picturing ancient craftsmen and markets. I had learned that Darius the Great was a renowned and benevolent ruler from the Achaemenid Dynasty, known for his building projects that helped fortify his vast empire and enhance trade throughout. I had also seen in his history books that the 'eternal flames' fuelled by natural gas seeps were sometimes considered sacred sites, with fire temples built nearby.

'But Father, how did they know it was so valuable?' I asked, my young voice tinged with the thrill of discovery.

Father chuckled softly. 'They knew because it made their lives easier, and anything that does so becomes precious. But it wasn't until much later that the world realised just how precious.'

He leaned closer, his voice dropping to a conspiratorial whisper. 'Then came explorers from distant lands, lured by whispers of our riches. They saw in our oil and gas not just the familiar uses, but the potential to fuel machines and engines, a power unlike any before. It was a treasure that nations would covet.'

The room seemed to shrink around them, the walls echoing with the weight of history. Father's hand rested gently on my shoulder. 'And that, my son, is why we must understand our past – to navigate our future.'

Outside Tehran's skyline twinkled under the dusky hue of twilight. The study suddenly became much brighter as a trusted servant turned on the lights, bathing the driveway, pool and garden in yellowish light from tungsten lamps. Father waved a hand in the air.

'All our electricity is generated from oil and gas reserves. The millions of motor vehicles out there are all powered by petroleum refined from crude oil. Imagine, a land rich yet untouched, its wealth hidden beneath the earth. In the early 1900s, a British man named William Knox D'Arcy believed in the potential buried in our lands. He obtained a concession that would change the face of our country forever.'

Caught up in the tale, I leaned forward. 'What did he do, Father?'

'D'Arcy gambled his fortune on the promise of oil. He faced years of hardships, drilling into the heart of our deserts and mountains with little to show. Many thought him a fool, chasing shadows.'

'And then?' my question was a whisper, barely over the soft breeze.

'Then, in a small town called Masjid-i-Suleiman, his team struck oil, and it was as if the earth itself was rewarding his persistence. This discovery wasn't just oil; it was a torrent of possibilities.'

I absorbed every word, my imagination fired by the tale of determination and discovery. 'So, he was right all along?'

'Yes, he was. But the story of oil is like the oil itself – rich and complex. It brought wealth and progress but also challenges and changes that we are still navigating today.'

Their dialogue lingered in the air, a blend of history and life lessons, as the night deepened around them, wrapping the city in its embrace.

The next day, I hammered on my father's office door, wanting to hear the rest of the story.

'Following D'Arcy's success, the stakes were higher, and the need for a structured approach became evident. In 1909, the Anglo–Persian Oil Company was formed, marking a new era in the oil industry.'

'Was it just about making money, Father?' I asked.

Father chuckled softly. 'It was about more than that. It was about power, about securing a resource that would become crucial to the entire world. The British government soon realised this and invested heavily in the company, ensuring a supply of oil for their navy, which was moving away from coal power.'

'The great ships of the sea powered by our oil as well?' I asked, his eyes wide with wonder.

'Exactly,' Jalil affirmed, nodding. 'And aeroplanes. And just about every machine you will see.'

'But Anglo–Persian Oil wasn't without its challenges. The company faced numerous obstacles, from logistical issues to political resistance within Iran. The path to progress is never smooth, as you will learn.'

Jalil's lessons always came with a mix of history and wisdom, teaching me not just the facts but the morals within them. 'Every entrepreneur faces resistance. Remember, it's not just about the challenges but how you respond to them that defines your path.'

As the night grew deeper, their conversation wove through the complexities of the early oil industry, like the intricate patterns of a Persian carpet under their feet. Each thread told a story of ambition, conflict, and the relentless pursuit of progress, laying the groundwork for my understanding of not just his family's legacy but also the broader world stage on which it unfolded.

As dusk settled over Tehran, painting the sky in hues of orange and purple, Father and I went up to the sit on the veranda, a gentle breeze stirring the air. With a contemplative look, we decided to discuss a pivotal moment in Iran's oil history – nationalisation.

'In 1951,' Jalil began, his voice heavy with history, 'Iran took a bold step. Our parliament voted to nationalise the Anglo–Persian Oil Company, which had been controlled by foreign powers for decades.'

'What happened next?' I asked.

'It triggered a major international crisis,' he explained. 'The British, heavily impacted, imposed an embargo on Iranian oil, crippling our economy.'

I frowned, the complexity of the situation sinking in. 'So, what came of it?'

Jalil sighed, picking his words carefully. 'Negotiations followed, but a lasting agreement wasn't reached until 1953. A consortium of international oil companies, including those from Britain and America, took over operations. Iran retained ownership of the oil, but the consortium managed production. However, tensions between the government and the shah were already high. The nationalisation further strained that relationship, and the situation culminated in a CIA-backed coup that toppled Prime Minister Mossadegh. Our experiment in democracy came to an end, and the shah regained control of the country.'

I was silent for a moment. 'Take me through it again, please,' I asked. Eventually, I sat back. 'That's quite a story,' I declared.

'It is,' Jalil affirmed. 'It was a lesson in sovereignty and the importance of controlling our resources. It taught us that while the path to autonomy is fraught with challenges, the fight for what's rightfully ours is always worth it.'

'You see, the discovery and exploitation of oil have not just changed our landscape; they have redefined our position on the global stage.'

Intrigued, I leaned closer. 'How so, Father?'

Father glanced at a framed photograph of Tehran from decades past, then back at his son. 'Oil brought wealth, certainly, but it also brought foreign interests and complexities that shaped our policies and our independence. It's a double-edged sword. On one hand, it funded our modernisation; on the other, it made us a focal point in international politics.'

Father continued, his gaze now fixed on a slowly spinning globe on his desk. 'The coup in '53, the nationalisation battles … they were all influenced by this black gold.'

Absorbing every word, I finally spoke, 'And what of the future, Father? How do you see this legacy affecting us moving forward?'

His hand paused on the globe, his fingers tracing the borders of Iran. 'The future, my son, will be about balancing growth with sovereignty. We've seen the power of oil, but it's time we also harness the power of our people, their creativity and resilience. That's the true wealth of a nation.'

As the conversation drifted into the evening, I felt a renewed sense of responsibility towards its future. Father's words were not just a lesson in history but a roadmap for the stewardship of Iran's resources, one that I would carry with me as I stepped into the world beyond Tehran.

Under the soft glow of the study's lamp, Father shared a more global perspective. Leaning over a map strewn across the table, his finger traced the intricate web of countries connected by the oil industry.

'Oil has not just shaped our nation,' he said. 'It has also woven us into the fabric of global geopolitics. We are now players on a much larger stage, whether we chose it or not.'

'Do you think that's a good thing, Father?' I asked.

'It's complex,' he admitted, smoothing the map with his hand. 'It brings prosperity, yes, but it also brings scrutiny and, at times, conflict. Our oil has made us wealthy, but it has also made us targets.'

He pointed to a series of lines indicating oil pipelines. 'These are not just routes for transporting oil, but also paths that carry with them geopolitical strategies and alliances. Every country that depends on our oil also holds a stake in our stability and decisions.'

I nodded, understanding the weight of such realities. 'So, our future is tied to how well we manage these relationships and our resources?'

'Exactly,' Father affirmed, with a mixture of pride and seriousness. 'Remember those words. *The future is tied to how well we manage our relationships and our resources.* This does not just apply to geopolitics, but also to ourselves on a personal level, to education, to our business dealings, to our lives. The challenge for your generation will be navigating these waters wisely, ensuring that Iran not only contributes to the world but also stands strong and respected in its own right.'

A BOOMING CITY

With the keen eye of youth, I marvelled at the kaleidoscope of modernity and tradition unfolding before me as Father drove across Tehran. 'Father, look how fast everything changes,' I remarked as we passed newly constructed high-rises that stood in stark contrast to the sprawling bazaars and shops around them.

Father smiled. 'Yes, the city grows like a sapling into a mighty tree. It's our past mingling with the promise of tomorrow. These streets are not just pathways of stone and tar, but of progress and challenge.'

As we continued, the architectural marvels spoke volumes of a city in transition. Skyscrapers reached for the clouds, casting long shadows over the traditional mud-brick homes that had once dominated the landscape. The air was filled with the sounds of construction, the clattering of tools and the shouts of workers layering the city's soundtrack.

'This is just the beginning,' Father explained, gesturing towards a busy construction site. 'Tehran is carving out a place on the world stage, and we're here to witness it, to be part of it.'

My eyes sparkled with the reflection of Tehran's aspirations, my mind racing with dreams of my own future amidst the burgeoning pulse of my hometown. We stopped at the Grand Bazaar, where the past and present of Iran coalesced. Wide-eyed and curious, I walked alongside Father through the labyrinth of stalls and shops. 'Every corner tells a story, son,' he told me, as we passed under arches that had stood for centuries, their stones worn smooth by countless passers-by.

The bazaar was not just a marketplace but the pulsating heart of Tehran's social and economic life. Vendors hawked spices that filled the air with pungent aromas, colourful textiles draped over stalls, and the glitter of gold and silver jewellery caught the eye from every angle.

'See how the merchants negotiate? It's an art, a dance of words and gestures,' Father explained, as we stopped to watch a seasoned vendor expertly barter with a customer over a finely woven carpet. 'This place has seen traders and travellers from all the roads of the Silk Route. It's more than a market; it's a historical archive of our culture and commerce.'

Just beyond lay more subdued but equally charming local markets and shops near our home, where the atmosphere was markedly different – a close-knit community where everyone knew each other's names and stories.

'Father, why do the shopkeepers always know what you're going to buy before you say anything?' I asked as we walked through their local market.

Father chuckled, patting my shoulder. 'Here, relationships matter just as much as the goods being sold. Mr Hosseini, the grocer, has seen you grow from a boy who loved sweet pastries to one who now helps pick the ripest fruits for Mother.'

As they passed Hosseini's stand, laden with fresh produce, the grocer called out, 'Ah, Jalil! I have the cherries you asked for last week. Perfectly sweet, just how your wife likes them.'

Father nodded appreciatively. 'Thank you, my friend. You always remember.'

This personal touch defined the local markets. Unlike the sprawling bazaar's anonymous crowds, here exchanges were filled with personal anecdotes and laughter. The fishmonger next door would tease me about my attempts at fishing and the tailor would ask about the family's wellbeing as he meticulously measured fabric.

'This is what makes our neighbourhood special,' said Father. 'The Grand Bazaar may have everything one could imagine, but here, it's about more than just transactions. It's about community.'

I also visited the shah's palace, an edifice of sheer grandeur and a testament to Iran's imperial past, with its extensive gardens and intricate design, dominating the cityscape; a constant reminder of the shah's presence and power. It was within shouting distance of our home, yet this school trip was my first visit. I marvelled at the towering columns and lavish decorations. 'It's like stepping into a different world,' I whispered to Saeed.

'Yes, but each stone here tells a story of our country's history, some of glory, others of strife,' replied Saeed.

As we walked through the palace, a guide pointed out the blend of Persian and Western architectural influences, highlighting the shah's ambitions to modernise Iran while preserving its cultural heritage. Beyond the palace, Tehran boasted other architectural marvels. Our guide took us to key religious buildings, such as the Grand Mosque with its majestic dome and minarets that pierced the city's skyline. We viewed governmental buildings, modern in design but no less impressive, each reflecting the era's push towards a new Tehran.

'These buildings,' the guide explained as they stood in front of the newly constructed city hall, 'represent our progress as a nation, our journey from the past into a future we're still shaping.'

One crisp autumn morning, Father took me to Tehran's National Gallery. In the serene atmosphere, I stood in contemplation before an array of Persian masterpieces. The curator, a refined woman in her late fifties, greeted Father as if he was a valued patron of the arts. She then turned to me, guiding me through the exhibits. 'This particular piece,' she gestured towards a vibrant miniature painting, 'dates back to the Safavid era, renowned for its intricate brushwork and rich colours.'

Intrigued, I leaned closer. 'The detail is extraordinary. It's like each stroke tells a part of our history,' I mused.

'Yes,' the curator nodded, adjusting her glasses. 'Art like this not only reflects aesthetic perfection but also serves as a conduit to our past.' She led him towards a modern sculpture, a stark contrast to the traditional paintings. 'And here we see a contemporary artist's interpretation of cultural evolution.'

I circled the sculpture, my curiosity piqued. 'It's fascinating to see how the old and new merge, each piece challenging our perceptions of beauty and tradition.'

The curator smiled, pleased with my understanding. 'Exactly. That's the essence of our collection – bridging epochs through art, making the old resonate with the new.'

As we continued our tour, I felt enriched, each artwork adding layers to my understanding of Iranian culture and identity.

We also visited Tehran's National Museum, which was very imposing. The guide, a scholarly man with deep-set eyes, shared tales of each artefact. 'This bronze mirror,' he pointed, 'is from the

Achaemenid period. It's not merely reflective glass but a symbol of the Zoroastrian belief in honesty and self-reflection.'

I leaned in. 'It's remarkable how these objects carry the weight of our ancestors' lives and beliefs.'

'Indeed,' the guide agreed, his voice echoing slightly in the vaulted room. 'Each item here tells a story of ingenuity and survival, like this clay tablet. It's one of the earliest examples of written communication, showcasing the administrative skills of our forebears.'

I ran my fingers lightly over the display case, reverent. 'It's humbling, isn't it? To stand so close to the roots of our history?'

The guide nodded, leading me towards a massive statue. 'Absolutely. And this piece,' he gestured, 'is thought to have guarded the gates of a lost palace. Imagine the tales it would tell if it could speak.'

The following weekend, Father announced that he had tickets for a concert for our family. The concert hall was vast, the ambience tranquil. I sat next to Mother, the plush velvet under my palms a stark contrast to the hard stone of the museums I'd toured a week ago. The stage was bathed in soft light, the orchestra tuning their instruments, a harmonious prelude to the evening's performance.

'I've always felt that music unlocks emotions in a way words simply can't,' I remarked to my mum, my eyes reflecting the stage lights.

She nodded sagely. 'Absolutely. Each note, each pause carries its own narrative. You'll see tonight how this orchestra tells a story without uttering a single word.'

As the conductor raised his baton, the conversation ceased, and the first notes drifted into the hall, enveloping the audience in a symphonic embrace. During the intermission, Mother leaned over, her voice low. 'Notice the violin's lament? It's as if it's mourning a long-lost love. Music, like the finest art, doesn't just entertain. It shapes us in ways we scarcely notice.'

We also visited one of Tehran's oldest mosques, its minarets towering gracefully against the clear blue sky.

'The architecture tells a story, doesn't it?' Father remarked, his eyes tracing the intricate tile work that adorned the façade.

'It does,' I replied, my gaze following Father's. 'Each pattern, each dome, is built with such precision and meaning. The tiles and mosaics are so beautiful.'

Inside, the mosque was a haven of tranquillity. The imam, spotting our interest, approached us, a gentle smile on his face. 'Welcome,' he said, his voice echoing softly through the vast prayer hall. 'This place is not just for worship, but for reflection, for community.'

I nodded, moved by the serene atmosphere. 'It feels like stepping out of time,' I observed.

'And into peace,' Father added, our conversation a whisper among the murmurs of other visitors and the soft footfalls on carpeted floors.

Later, seeking a change from the spiritual to the natural, we visited one of Tehran's renowned parks. Here, the city's hustle faded into the background, replaced by the rustling of leaves and the laughter of children playing.

'This is the city's breath,' Father said as we strolled along a tree-lined path, the foliage a burst of gold and red above them. 'Places like this offer respite for the soul.'

'Yes, a moment to recharge,' I agreed, taking a deep breath of the crisp air. 'It's amazing how such spaces can exist amid the chaos of the city.'

The walk continued, each step a further exploration of Tehran's diverse cultural landscape, a blend of reverence and relaxation that defined our home city. Shops boasting the latest Western fashions were shoulder to shoulder with traditional bazaars, creating a mosaic of the old and new.

'See how the city morphs,' Father mused, gesturing towards a sleek new building rising beside an ancient mosque. 'It's our heritage entwining with the new world. It's like watching two eras merge on the same streets.' The contrast was striking, with modern cafés filled with young, stylish Tehranis sipping coffee next to tea houses where older men played backgammon and discussed politics under the watchful eyes of portraits of the shah.

As we continued our walk, we discussed how Tehran, once a historical stronghold, was rapidly growing into a cosmopolitan hub, attracting not only tourists but also international businesses. Tehran was carving out a new identity, one that embraces both its rich history and its future aspirations.

Our tour ended in one of Tehran's parks, a green oasis where families gathered to enjoy their surroundings, seemingly untouched by the rapid urbanisation around them. Father nodded towards the crowds. 'Do you see,' he asked, 'the young woman in a trendy miniskirt and a colourful blouse?'

I did see, but before I could answer, Father continued, 'And to her right, an older woman in a *chador*, a full-body black veil, accompanied by, probably, her younger daughter, wearing a *hijab*, a stylish modern headscarf.'

To our right, a man in a crisp Western suit and ties, standing next to another in a *deraa,* a traditional long robe, and another in a *chakman*, a long-sleeved coat reaching below his knees. By the coffee shop stood students in jeans. Father said this was part of Shah Mohammad Reza Pahlavi's push for modernisation: a relaxed, tolerant society, a wonderful blend of traditional and Western cultures promoting learning, business, peace, and harmony and helping us to become rich, both spiritually and financially.

Even at my young age, I could see what he meant. The city was full of beautiful contrasts, old and new existing side by side. 'It's like life, isn't it?' Father said. 'This should prepare you for a world that's equally layered, where understanding different perspectives is not just useful, but necessary.'

As the evening deepened, my thoughts turned towards the legacy of Tehran. The city, with all its complexity and challenges, had a way of seeping into me, shaping me without me realising it. Its richness in culture and history left a mark on everyone.

His father raised his glass, his eyes reflecting the city lights. 'To Tehran, a city of timeless lessons and endless possibilities.'

'To Tehran,' I echoed, my heart full of both nostalgia and hope. No matter where life took me, the imprint of my home city would forever guide my steps.

ENTREPRENEURIAL ROOTS

My fascination with business sparked early, kindled by the bustling markets and Father's successful entrepreneurial ventures. I watched intently as he negotiated deals, his keen sense managing to weave prosperity from the threads of everyday transactions. One evening, as we walked through the crowded marketplace, he pointed to the throngs of buyers and sellers. 'Each person here plays a part in this commerce,' he said. 'Learn to watch, listen, and understand their needs, and you can find your place among them.'

Absorbing every word, I felt the pulse of the city fuel my aspirations. 'I want to start something of my own, Baba,' I ventured, my eyes reflecting the myriad of lantern lights flickering across the market.

Jalil looked at me, pride in his eyes: 'And you shall, my boy. But remember, a true entrepreneur listens first – to the market, to the people. Your time will come, and you'll be ready.'

Inspired by Father's wisdom and the dynamic energy of Tehran, I began to dream of my own business, imagining a venture that would allow me to step into the role of the merchants I admired. Aged just ten yet brimming with a budding entrepreneur's zeal, I formed a plan, and decided to enlist Ishmael, the son of the Hashtroudi residence's gardener. Ishmael was tall and had a distinctive appearance, which we would joke about, but he was a delightful young man only a couple of years older than me.

I proposed my plan to Ishmael beneath the thick branches of a robust tree, our makeshift office.

'Ishmael, let's start our own venture. We'll sell chilled soft drinks right here. I'll manage the finances from my savings, and you handle the day-to-day operations.'

He nodded. 'That sounds brilliant. But how will we keep the drinks cool in this heat?'

I grinned. 'We'll buy a block of ice daily and wrap it in a sack to keep the bottles cold. It's simple yet effective.' Together, we strategised the logistics, deciding to source popular sodas including Coca-Cola and Canada Dry from the nearest wholesaler, based three miles away in the Tajrish Bazaar.

The next day, we set up our stall under the tree's welcoming shade. A rustic wooden table served as our counter, with bottles neatly arranged and a massive ice block wrapped in hessian, glistening as it slowly melted. The set-up was modest but inviting, drawing the attention of passers-by who appreciated a cold drink in the Tehran heat.

As the sun climbed higher, so did their spirits. Ishmael handled the sales with a charm that drew customers, while I kept meticulous track of every bottle sold and the dwindling ice. Their teamwork was seamless, each playing to his strength, turning a simple idea into a bustling little business that buzzed with the energy of their combined aspirations and hard work.

Early in the morning, Ishmael and I prepared for another busy day at our soft drink stand. As the sun began to warm the streets of Tehran, we arranged the chilled bottles neatly, anticipating the rush of thirsty customers.

'Make sure we keep the ice thick around the sodas,' Ishmael remarked, checking the hessian sack's dampness. 'It's going to be another scorcher today.'

As the day unfolded, a variety of customers stopped by – taxi drivers grabbing a quick drink, workers on their lunch breaks, and even a few curious tourists. Each interaction was a learning opportunity. 'Watch how the taxi drivers always take an extra bottle for the road,' I pointed out. 'Let's think about offering a "buy two, get a discount" deal tomorrow.'

Ishmael agreed. 'That's a good idea. It could speed up our sales and increase our turnover before the ice melts.'

Midday brought a small crisis when we discovered that a batch of sodas hadn't been chilled long enough. 'We need a quick fix, or we'll lose customers!' Ishmael panicked.

Calmly, I thought for a moment, then said, 'Let's rearrange the stock. Move the colder bottles to the front and rotate them more frequently. We'll tell our customers it's a fresh batch, just in.'

The strategy worked seamlessly, and the flow of customers remained steady. As we tallied up our earnings at day's end, the lessons of entrepreneurship were not just in the profit but in the camaraderie and quick thinking that defined the venture.

On a sweltering summer day, we also had to deal with the sudden appearance of a new soft drink vendor just down the street. I noticed the dwindling number of customers as the new stand boasted a large, modern cooler.

'This could cut deep into our profits,' Ishmael observed, worry etching his features.

I remembered something my father often said: 'In business, when faced with competition, innovate or offer something they cannot.' Inspired, I proposed, 'Why don't we offer a loyalty card? Buy nine drinks, get the tenth free.' It was something I had heard Dad talk about.

We quickly made simple cards from spare cardboard, marking slots to be punched with each purchase. As customers returned, intrigued by the novelty and promise of a free drink, word spread. Even new customers decided to give our stand a try, drawn by the promise of a reward.

'Our cooling might not last all day, but our customers' memories of rewards will,' I said, a grin spreading across his face as he watched a satisfied customer walk away, loyalty card in hand.

The move not only countered the immediate threat but also strengthened our connection with regulars, who appreciated the personal touch. It not only alleviated the crisis but also infused the business with a renewed sense of community and customer loyalty.

Over the next few summers, our soft drinks venture flourished. We smartly reinvested our profits into improving the stand, adding more variety to our offerings and investing in a portable cooler to keep the drinks chilled longer, enhancing their appeal on the hottest days.

'One day, we'll have the best stand in all of Tehran,' I declared confidently as we counted the day's earnings.

Ishmael laughed, clapping me on the back. 'With your ideas and our hard work, I don't doubt it.'

Our small venture not only boosted my understanding of business operations but also solidified my resolve to pursue bigger dreams. Each successful summer cemented my belief in the power of innovation and customer service.

'It's not just selling drinks, Ishmael. It's about creating something people trust and return to,' I explained one evening as we planned future enhancements.

The success also deepened our bond. Ishmael, now more like a brother, shared in the triumphs and challenges, each obstacle overcome drawing us closer.

This collaboration taught me valuable lessons about resilience, strategic planning, and the importance of nurturing relationships: lessons that would guide me in future endeavours.

'I never thought selling drinks would teach me so much about the world,' I mused one evening, sharing a quiet moment with Ishmael as we began to pack up our stand for the day.

Years later, news reached me of Ishmael's death during the Iran–Iraq War. The shock was profound. Nothing, it seemed, was permanent.

'Life is fragile, just like our ice blocks under the sun,' I reflected in sorrow.

This early venture imparted crucial life lessons: the value of hard work, the importance of innovation and the impact of genuine human connections. To these I added other wisdoms, such as the courage and negotiation I learned from Father when dealing with a reluctant debtor. On one brisk autumn morning, he had enlisted my help for a delicate task. 'Today, you will learn a valuable lesson in handling difficult situations,' he told me.

As we approached a well-known shoe manufacturer's shop, Father paused, his hand on my shoulder. 'Go inside and ask for Mr Hakopian. Tell him something interesting waits for him outside.'

Nervous yet eager to please Father, I did as I was asked. Inside, there was a woman who was reluctant to call Mr Hakopian. I explained that I needed to pass on information in private and was not allowed to tell her about it. Eventually she went out to the back and returned with the man, a stern-looking fellow who was initially resistant. 'Sir, there's something outside that might interest you,' I ventured, trying to mimic my father's confidence.

Curiosity piqued; Mr Hakopian followed me outside. To his surprise, Father was waiting by his car, papers in hand. The confrontation that followed was a masterclass in negotiation. 'Mr Hakopian, we have extended enough courtesy. It's time to settle your accounts,' Father stated, his tone firm yet polite.

I saw how Father was using strategy over strength, a lesson that later shaped my own approach to business. Seeing Father handle that situation taught me more about respect and power than any business class could.

Such lessons prepared me for my own challenges ahead, blending the practical with the profound. I had no idea that the lessons I was learning would prove to be so important for my future.

CHAPTER NINE:
THRILLS AND SPILLS

In the quiet warmth of the Hashtroudi living room one day in the mid-1960s, Mother and Father gathered us together for a family meeting that was to chart the course of our futures. The room took on a solemn air as Father cleared his throat, his eyes sweeping over his children with a blend of solemnity and pride.

'Today,' he began, his voice steady but tinged with emotion, 'we stand on the brink of a new chapter. Massoud, Hedi, Nadereh, you have been given an opportunity to continue your education abroad.'

Mother, sitting beside him, held a comforting smile, though her eyes mirrored the storm of emotions brewing inside her. The children, sensing the gravity of the moment, exchanged anxious glances.

'In a few weeks,' Jalil continued, 'Massoud and Hedi will join a boarding school in Sussex in the south of England, and Nadereh, you will head to Geneva. This wasn't an easy decision, but your mother and I believe this is a crucial step for your futures.'

The room filled with a heavy silence as the siblings absorbed the news. Massoud nodded slowly, his expression resolute. Hedi looked thoughtful, perhaps slightly overwhelmed, while Nadereh's face was lit with a mix of excitement and nervousness.

'I know this will be a big change,' Father added, his voice softening, 'but remember, you are not just carrying your dreams but also the hopes of your family. You will learn things far beyond what Tehran can offer, and in doing so, you will bring that knowledge back home, enriching not only yourselves but also your country.'

Mother, squeezing Father's hand, spoke in a whisper of strength. 'We have raised you with love and values that will guide you through any challenge. Always remember who you are and where you come from, no matter how far you go.'

As the meeting drew to a close, they stood to embrace each child, whispering words of encouragement and love. The significance of the moment was not lost on anyone. This was not just about educational opportunities; it was about stepping into a wider world, carrying the legacy of our family in every step.

Over the following weeks, the Hashtroudi household became a hub of preparation. Trunks and suitcases lay open in every conceivable space, their gaping maws gradually filling with neatly folded clothes, books, and personal keepsakes. Mother and Father moved through these preparations with a practiced air of efficiency, yet each item packed was a silent testament to the impending distances that would soon separate them.

As second youngest, I found myself weaving through this orchestrated chaos, absorbing the mixed emotions that permeated the air. Watching my older siblings, each caught up in their own whirlwind of anticipation and apprehension, I couldn't help but feel a twinge of envy and loneliness. My role had suddenly shifted; from mischief-maker and centre of attention, I was now an observer left behind.

'I'll need these notes,' Massoud declared one afternoon, sifting through stacks of textbooks and papers. 'Can't risk falling behind before I even start.'

Hedi was quieter, his usual humour subdued as he folded his clothes and arranged them into his section of the trunk. 'Do you think they'll like me there?' he asked.

Unsure how to comfort my brother, I offered a shrug. 'They'd be stupid not to,' I said, forcing a grin.

Mother, ever the sentinel of her family's emotions, watched these interactions with a keen eye, stepping in when the weight of farewells threatened to overwhelm, her words a soothing balm. 'Remember, you're carrying a piece of home with you,' she reminded my siblings as she helped Nadereh select which dresses to take. 'And home will always be here, waiting for your return.'

As the day of departure neared, the house was filled with last-minute visitors – relatives, friends, and neighbours – each bringing gifts and well-wishes. The laughter and chatter, usually the lifeblood of the home, now felt like echoes of a soon-to-be-distant normalcy. On the final night, the family gathered for a farewell dinner. The table was laden with favourite dishes, a feast meant to celebrate but tinged with the sorrow of imminent parting. Father raised his glass, his voice steady but his eyes glistening. 'To new beginnings,' he toasted. 'May they bring you joy and success.'

As they ate, the conversation flowed around memories and hopes, the laughter mingling with the clink of cutlery. I watched my siblings, memorising their faces, their laughter, storing these moments like treasures. I knew that tomorrow everything would change, that the morning would bring a quiet unlike any before.

That night, as I lay in bed, the sounds of my siblings packing their final items punctuated the quiet. The reality of their departure hung over me like a shadow. Tomorrow, I would wake up to a quieter house, a slower pace. But tonight, I listened to familiar sounds, a lullaby of the life they had known, a life that was about to change.

The morning dawned with a solemnity that permeated the household, marking the departure of Massoud, Hedi, and Nadereh. The usual morning activity was replaced by a quiet, meticulous attention to every detail, from the final packing of luggage to the sombre breakfast that no one seemed to have an appetite for. Mother and Father moved through these rituals with a bittersweet precision, their smiles forced, their touches lingering.

Witnessing the gravity of the day, I felt an unfamiliar tightness in my chest as I watched my siblings make final checks on their belongings. My role as the observer, the youngest, not leaving but rather watching as my world shifted, became painfully clear. I was struck by the weight of what this departure meant – not just miles apart, but continents away.

As they loaded the car, the air was thick with unspoken words and suppressed emotions. The drive to the airport was quiet, each family member lost in their thoughts, the landscape blurring past as they neared their first major goodbye.

Arriving at the airport, I felt a surge of excitement despite the sadness. It was my first time at such a place and I watched in awe as planes took off and landed, marvelling at the roaring engines and sleek fuselages. But the awe couldn't mask the dread of the impending farewells.

At the check-in, the finality began to sink in. Nadereh clung to Mother, her eyes brimming with tears, while Massoud and Hedi tried to maintain a stoic demeanour, failing occasionally as their voices cracked with emotion. Father stood firm, offering words of encouragement and pride, his hand firmly on my shoulder.

The walk to the departure gate was the longest I had ever taken. Each step seemed to echo in my heart, a stark reminder that the siblings I had grown up with would soon be beyond my reach. At the gate, the final hugs were exchanged, each embrace a little longer and tighter.

'I'm proud of you all,' Father's voice broke through the thick emotional air as he hugged each of his children. 'Remember who you are and remember that home is always here, waiting.'

Mother, with a trembling smile, managed to whisper, 'Take care of each other,' her hands cupping their faces, memorising each feature.

I felt a mix of pride and profound loneliness as I hugged my siblings. 'Make us all proud,' I managed to say, at barely a whisper.

The family stood in silence as the siblings disappeared from view. The return to the now emptier car was quiet, each member lost in their thoughts, the absence of three pivotal figures setting in. I gazed out the window, the airport fading into the distance, feeling one chapter close and a new, uncertain one beginning. The ride home was silent, the air filled with reflections and unspoken fears about the future, each heart privately nursing its wounds of separation, yet clinging to the hope of reunion.

The household felt eerily silent in the following days; the absence of the laughter and ceaseless energy that my missing brothers and sister brought to every room was palpable. I found myself wandering through the corridors, each step echoing off the walls, a constant reminder of the void their leaving had created. My room, once a hub of shared secrets and late-night discussions, now seemed too large, too quiet. The loneliness was a tangible presence, weighing heavily. The dinner table now had too many empty seats.

Mother spent more time in the kitchen, cooking elaborate meals that no one had the heart to eat. The aroma of Persian spices filled the house, a desperate attempt to bring back a sense of normalcy. Yet, her eyes often betrayed her, glossy with unshed tears when she thought no-one was looking. Father buried himself in work. His days at the office stretched longer, and when he was home, his mind seemed preoccupied, his thoughts miles away with his children. Yet, he made a conscious effort to spend more time with me, perhaps understanding better than anyone the depth of my solitude.

Each weekend, Father took me to cultural and historical sites around Tehran in a bid to fill the silence with the city's heritage. The rides home were often silent, with each of us lost in our own thoughts. I appreciated these efforts but felt a growing detachment from the child I used to be, the one who had not yet known such profound loss. I missed the noise, arguments and laughter that my siblings had brought into my life. Our house, with its opulent rooms and lush gardens, felt less like a home and more like a museum. Mother began to organise small gatherings with relatives and friends. These evenings brought some relief, the chatter and laughter a balm to their collective melancholy. Yet, the moment the guests left, the silence returned, more profound and more poignant.

One evening, as my parents and I sat in the living room listening to classical Persian music, Father spoke up. 'We are a family,' he said softly, 'and we will find our way through this together. It's what those who have left would want for us.'

These words, meant to comfort, seemed to echo around the room, a reminder of the enduring bond they shared, unbroken by distance. I looked at my parents, their faces etched with a mixture of strength and sadness, and felt a surge of love and gratitude. I knew then that while the shape of our family might have changed, the foundation on which it was built remained unshakeable. The resilience they displayed, the way they clung to each other, taught me more than anything else could about love and family.

As the seasons passed, the family slowly adapted to their new reality. Mother and Father gradually established routines that filled the gaps left by their absent children, while I, now the eldest at home, found myself assuming new responsibilities, helping more around the house and taking an even keener interest in the family business.

The change in me was palpable. I matured faster, my conversations bearing a depth inspired by my newfound responsibilities and the weight of my siblings' absence. Father fostered my growth with gentle guidance, while Mother reinvented her daily activities to cope with the loneliness. She started attending more community events and social gatherings, establishing a network of friends and acquaintances that brought new energy into her life. These connections not only helped fill the silence in the home but also brought new stories and laughter to the dinner table.

The family also evolved its communication practices to maintain close ties with Massoud, Hedi, and Nadereh. The advent of more accessible international calls and letters adorned with tales of foreign lands became a beacon of joy, as each letter was read and re-read, its contents shared and discussed.

Celebrations and festivals, once vibrant family affairs, now carried a bittersweet tone. Yet, Mother and Father made sure to include the essence of their children's new experiences abroad into these occasions, integrating stories and foreign customs into their traditional practices.

As I prepared for the future, the lessons of resilience, adaptability, and the enduring strength of family bonds shaped my outlook. The separation affected us all, but also underscored the unwavering support system we had in each other – a foundation strong enough to withstand changes brought by time and distance.

More than ever, I felt a deep connection to my parents' aspirations and the sacrifices they had made. I promised myself to uphold the values instilled by my parents – resilience, education, and a recognition of the importance of family.

A CLASSICAL SCHOOLING

After Massoud, Hedi, and Nadereh left, my parents sought a prestigious local alternative for me, enrolling me at Khwarizmi Secondary School. Named after the renowned Persian mathematician Muhammad ibn Musa al-Khwarizmi, the school stood as a testament to a legacy of scholarly excellence. Al-Khwarizmi was also the father of algebra – a term derived from 'Al-Jabr', one of his ground-breaking works around AD 820. His Latinised name, Algoritmi, led to the term 'algorithm', revolutionising mathematical thought and computation.' He was pivotal in introducing the Hindu–Arabic numeral system to the West, including the concept of zero – a figure the Romans never conceived.

The school, one of the best in Tehran, was stricter and focused more on academic studies than Roshdiah. Initially, I struggled, but later adjusted, with the guidance of a strict but effective mathematics teacher. On my first day, I stood at the school gates, my heart thumping with anticipation and nervousness. The towering façade of the school loomed, its historic walls echoing with the whispers of a thousand past scholars. I couldn't help but feel a surge of excitement about the adventures lying ahead.

'Remember,' said Father, his voice steady and encouraging, 'every challenge here is a stepping stone to your future. You're ready for this. The teachers here will demand excellence, but I know you can rise to it. Make us proud, son.'

Left to navigate the new school alone, my first challenge was finding my classroom. I approached a group of students, my voice slightly hesitant. 'Excuse me, could you help me find room 102?'

A tall boy with a friendly grin responded, 'Sure, you're in my class. I'm Farhad.' We set off down the hall. By the time we reached the classroom, I felt a bit more at ease, thanks to Farhad's easy camaraderie. I took a seat beside him, ready to face whatever the day held.

As I settled into my new school routine, I quickly discovered that the academic rigour was indeed more intense than at Roshdiah. Each day brought a fresh challenge, from complex mathematical problems to in-depth historical essays, pushing me to immerse myself in my studies. Yet, I found my stride, spurred on by a growing circle of friends and supportive teachers.

I admired Farhad's confidence and the easy way he progressed through school life, qualities he aspired to embody himself. It was during these conversations that I truly appreciated the diversity of thought and background his new school offered.

One significant aspect of this new life was the sports programme. I had always been keen on soccer, but this school's facilities and coaching were at another level. I found myself spending evenings on the field, practising dribbles and shots under the watchful eye of Coach Bahram, a former national player known for his rigorous training methods.

'Hashtroudi, focus on your form, not just power,' Coach Bahram would shout across the field. I took these lessons seriously, knowing that discipline in sport could translate to discipline in life.

The transition wasn't without its difficulties. The pressure to perform well academically and fit into this new environment weighed heavily on me. Sometimes, I felt overwhelmed, missing the familiarity of Roshdiah and the simpler challenges I had faced there.

'Did you ever feel out of place?' I asked Father tentatively.

'Many times,' he admitted with a smile. 'But, it's not about fitting in with everyone else. It's about finding your own path, learning from every experience, and growing stronger.'

I began to view each day as an opportunity, engaging more in class and volunteering for group projects. Slowly, the new school began to feel like a second home. As the year progressed, my confidence grew. I was no longer the new kid struggling to keep up but had become a valued member of my class, known for his keen insights and willingness to help others. My journey through the senior school was shaping me, not just academically but personally, laying the groundwork for the challenges I would one day face beyond its walls.

HEART ATTACK

Yet, a major shock was in store. In the relaxed atmosphere of an ordinary Thursday, Father suddenly suffered a heart attack, which, while not fatal, significantly affected his health. The Hashtroudi household was abruptly thrust into disarray. The day had begun like any other, with the morning rituals of breakfast and farewells as Father headed to his office near the Grand Bazaar. However, around midday, a frantic call from his office plunged the family into a state of emergency, propelling us into a race against time to get him to hospital.

Not yet a teenager, I felt the ground shift beneath me as I entered the hospital's stark, antiseptic corridors. Father, invincible in my eyes, now lay vulnerable under the harsh lights of the emergency room. The family gathered, whispers filled with worry and prayers, around Father's bed, where he, though weakened, offered a feeble smile that belied his discomfort.

'My boy,' he murmured, his voice barely a thread of sound. 'Always remember, strength isn't just physical. It's in the will to keep going, no matter what.'

These words, simple yet profound, etched themselves into my heart, shaping the resolve with which I approached the days. Every afternoon, after school, I made my way to the private hospital, my steps quickening as I navigated the familiar route. The hospital days stretched into an endless loop of sterile white walls and the dull hum of fluorescent lights. I trudged through the routine of visits, each one a blur of consultations and agonising waits. The ward, mostly quiet except for the rhythmic beeping from Father's room, could erupt at any moment. Muffled screams, a flurry of doctors in white coats, the frantic wail of a family – then an unsettling silence that pressed down heavier than before.

I spent afternoons glued to Father's side. Textbooks lay open in his lap, mostly untouched. The rhythmic beeping of the monitors was a constant companion, a stark reminder of the fragile state of the man I loved most. Conversation was strained. We tiptoed around the illness, a silent worry hanging heavy in the air. Father, knowing our worries, would dredge up stories from a past filled with grit and resilience. Tales of youthful scrapes and hard-won victories, a testament to the strength that flowed through our shared blood. These stories, even with their familiar comfort, couldn't quite dispel the deep current of worry with me, a fear I couldn't quite voice.

One particular evening, as the sun cast a golden glow through the hospital window, I listened intently as Father recounted his early days in Tehran, navigating the complexities of starting a business in the unpredictable vagaries of the city's economy. 'Every challenge was a lesson,' he said. 'Each setback taught me something vital about perseverance. These are the lessons I want to pass on to you.'

The family rallied around Father, and even my cousin Parvis flew back from the USA to visit and give support. As the passage of recovery unfolded, the family dynamics shifted. Mother, always a pillar of gentle strength, took on the logistical challenges with grace, coordinating between home and hospital, ensuring Father's comfort and the family's wellbeing. My younger sibling, aware of the tension but not fully grasping the gravity, found solace in my newfound steadiness.

Amidst the clinical routine, my journey was not just about facing Father's mortality but also discovering my own capacity for strength in vulnerability. One afternoon, as I sat beside Father, watching the gentle rise and fall of his chest, I felt a strong connection to my father's earlier lessons on resilience.

'Dad,' I ventured, my voice hesitant, 'how did you find the strength to start over, each time things didn't go as planned?'

Father turned to me, a spark of vigour in his eyes. 'It's about believing,' he said. 'Believe in yourself, in your dreams, and in the power of standing up after a fall. Never lose that belief, no matter how hard the path seems.'

This exchange stayed with me as I navigated my own future challenges. As Father's condition stabilised and the prospect of returning home became tangible, the family prepared to reintegrate into the rhythm of everyday life, forever changed by the ordeal, yet stronger for it. We knew the road ahead would hold more challenges, but the foundation laid during those hospital days – of unity, resilience, and profound love – promised that no hardship was too great to overcome together.

MOTORBIKE ADVENTURE

My own brush with hospitals in this period, was, in stark contrast, completely my own doing. In the pulsating heart of mid-1960s Tehran, the lure of freedom rode on two wheels: a motorbike promising adventure and escape. Barely thirteen, the sight of my peers zipping through the alleys of my neighbourhood on their gleaming machines kindled a burning desire within me.

'Everyone has one, Baba,' I pleaded one crisp morning, eyes wide with longing as group of boys my age sped past on their machines. The thrill of the motorbikes was palpable, their riders adorned with leather jackets and an air of daring I desperately wanted to emulate.

Father listened with a patient smile. 'A motorbike, hmm?' he mused, rubbing his chin thoughtfully. 'And what does your mother say?'

My face fell slightly. 'Maman doesn't like them,' I admitted. 'She worries too much.'

'She worries because she cares,' said Father, 'but let's see what we can do. Perhaps a little freedom is good for a young man.'

I repeated his plea every day until, to my surprise, Mother flew to England to visit my two brothers studying there. The house felt emptier, and the absence of Mother's cautious voice made my request seem less daunting. Seizing an opportunity, I approached Father again, with more determination.

'Now that Maman is not here, can we talk about the motorbike again?' I asked, my voice hopeful.

'All right,' said Father with a resigned chuckle. 'Go to my office tomorrow, and we'll discuss it there.'

The next day, my heart thumped as I navigated the familiar path. The streets of Tehran unfurled, exposing the babble of daily life, vibrant and ever-changing. Father greeted me with a nod, his expression unreadable. 'I've spoken to a few shops near the bazaar,' he began, handing me a slip of paper with several addresses. 'Go, look at the bikes, and choose one if you must.'

My eyes lit up. 'Really, Baba? You mean it?'

'Yes, but be wise about your choice. And remember, safety first.'

The motorbike shop was a cavern of wonders. The owner, forewarned by Father, welcomed me warmly. 'Your father mentioned you might be coming,' he said knowingly. 'Let's see what we have for you.'

I walked through rows of motorbikes, each model gleaming under the fluorescent lights, and selected a sleek, modestly powered bike.

'I'll take this one,' I declared, nervous and proud.

'Excellent choice,' the shop owner approved. 'I'll have it delivered to your home by this evening.'

Returning to Father's office, I could hardly sit still. 'It's done, Baba. I chose one,' I said.

Father raised an eyebrow, his look one of amusement and slight apprehension. 'Well, then, we shall see how it goes. But for now, take a seat and wait while I finish my work. Let's head home. Your new ride awaits.'

The time passed slowly. Eventually as the evening sun dipped below the horizon, casting long shadows over the Hashtroudi residence, a small truck manoeuvred carefully into our driveway. I watched, heart in throat, as workers unloaded my new motorbike. It was even more beautiful than I remembered, its surface catching the last rays of the setting sun. This was it, my very own motorbike. I ran my hands over the sleek metal, the feel of metal more satisfying than I had imagined.

Father tested me on the basics of ownership, maintenance, handling and road sense and made me circle inside the grounds using the driveway and footpaths, telling me to practise on the public road in the daylight of the next day, being careful to start in quiet areas.

'Yes, Baba,' I nodded earnestly, already dreaming of the roads I would explore.

The next day, the exhilaration of my first proper ride on my new motorbike was unmatched. The engine's rumble felt like a drumbeat propelling me into a world of untold adventures. It was early morning; the streets were nearly empty and Tehran was just beginning to stir.

I negotiated the streets with a cautious excitement. Each turn was a small victory, each stretch of road a new conquest. The wind against my face was chilling and exhilarating, filling me with a sense of boundless freedom. As I rode, the city unveiled itself in a different light, less intimidating and more inviting. The familiar paths to school, the local bazaar, and the sprawling parks unfolded with new nuances.

However, my new adventures quickly came unstuck. One afternoon a few months after acquiring the motorbike, a sudden swerve to avoid a stray dog led to a harsh tumble. The world spun wildly as I skidded across the pavement, the motorbike clattering beside me in a jarring symphony of scrapes.

When the world righted itself, I was sprawled on the ground, face pressed against the cool pavement. Pain throbbed through my body, and I couldn't move my jaw. I tried to call out, but my voice was muffled, my mouth barely opening. The realisation hit me hard; the accident was serious.

The aftermath was a blur of hospital visits, where the reality of my injuries set in. My jaw was severely injured, requiring weeks to heal properly. Soup and soft foods became my sustenance, as I couldn't chew without significant pain. The weight loss was rapid, my body shrinking as my face healed.

My motorbike stood untouched during those weeks; the joy it had brought overshadowed by the harsh lesson of vulnerability. Father handled the situation with a quiet strength. While he supported me through recovery, he also saw it as a crucial learning moment. He arranged for the motorbike to be returned to almost as-new condition, believing that once I recovered, the desire to ride would return, tempered with a newfound respect for the machine and the road.

The recovery process was not just physical but emotional. I had to come to terms with the fragility of life and the consequences of his choices. Mother, though deeply upset, was a constant presence by my side, her care a silent 'I told you so' that was both comforting and chastening.

In the midst of my recovery, a new regulation came into effect, mandating that all motorbikes must be registered and display a number plate. At Father's suggestion, I enlisted the help of Ismael to navigate the registration process. The plan was to go to the police station early and get the paperwork done, but reality proved more challenging. The lines were long, and the bureaucracy stifling, with the possibility of being turned away after hours of waiting.

Ismael, ever resourceful, suggested a workaround. Instead of enduring the endless queue, we approached the station's kitchen, where the police officers' meals were prepared. He knew someone there who brewed tea and coffee for the officers. With a mixture of charm and guile, we presented our case. The cook, amused and perhaps flattered by the direct approach, agreed to help, taking the documents and disappearing into the police station's administrative maze. Half an hour later, he returned, a smile on his face and a new number plate in his hand. The task was completed, not through the front door, but through the kitchen. It's sometimes not what you know, but who you know.

Reflecting on the saga, I realised how much I had grown. The lessons from my motorbike adventures remained with me, a foundation of resilience that I carried into adulthood. I had learned a little about the limits of freedom and the weight of responsibility. Every choice, every turn of the handlebars, was a step in the journey of life.

ARCHITECTING MY FUTURE

One quiet evening, Father began a conversation. 'There's going to be a new school in Tehran,' he said. 'A German technical college is opening its doors. It offers a course in architecture.'

'Architecture?' My interest was piqued instantly. I had a rapid recall of the silver, two-seater Mercedes sports car belonging to the architect of the summer villa in Challous, followed by thoughts of the city's skyline. He often sketched the minarets and modern buildings that dotted Tehran's landscape.

'It's not just about building structures. It's about envisioning spaces, imagining what could be,' Father explained, his eyes reflecting a visionary's passion, something that I had inherited. 'They also teach in English and German, which would be invaluable for your future.'

The prospect of studying architecture lit a new fire in me. I imagined designing buildings that would stand tall against Tehran's backdrop, perhaps even beyond Iran's borders. The discussions with Father were inspirational.

We held a little household celebration when I received the acceptance letter. 'This is your future,' said Mother. The college proved to be everything I had hoped for and more. The blend of technical precision and creative design fascinated me and I absorbed every lesson with eagerness. Classes were a mix of theory and practical application, often taking me to construction sites where blueprints came to life.

Friendships at the college were formed over shared drafting tables and complex project models. Discussions often stretched late into the night, whether in the college labs or over steaming cups of tea at a nearby café. These were not just peers: they were collaborators in a journey of discovery and creation.

As the months unfolded, my newfound academic rigour became a cornerstone of my daily life. Mornings were brisk with enthusiasm as I joined classmates in deciphering complex architectural designs and engineering principles. The integration of practical sessions with theoretical learning gave me a tangible sense of accomplishment, sparking a deeper appreciation for architecture.

Every lecture was an opportunity to connect dots from historical architectural marvels to modern design techniques, bridged by discussions that often spilled over into spirited debates during lunch breaks. My teachers, mostly German, brought a meticulousness to the coursework that both intimidated and inspired me. Their insistence on precision and depth pushed me to my limits and the curriculum's inclusion of English and German language courses added layers to my education, equipping me with tools needed in a rapidly globalising world. The school emphasised the importance of historical context in architecture, a theme that resonated deeply with me, following my visits to Iran's historical sites.

In a quiet corner of the college library, amidst the towering stacks of architectural journals and dusty tomes of design history, I found my sanctuary. There, under the soft glow of the reading lamps, I began to draft my first major project – a proposal for a community centre serving as a space for recreation and a hub of cultural exchange. The project became my passion, consuming evenings and weekends as I refined each line and curve of my drawings. My desk at college became cluttered with sketches and architectural models. I engaged deeply with my professors, seeking their advice and soaking up their feedback. These interactions were truly transformative, pushing me to think beyond the aesthetics of building to consider its social impact.

'Architecture is more than the creation of a space – it's the crafting of an environment that influences how people live and interact,' Professor Baum, one of my mentors, would often say. I took these words to heart, seeing in them a reflection of my father's teachings about the importance of community and connectivity.

The culmination of my efforts was presented at the end of the semester in a packed room of peers and faculty. With a model of the community centre on display, I articulated my design philosophy, emphasising sustainability and inclusivity. My presentation was met with enthusiastic applause.

Outside academic assignments, I also ventured into the architectural landscape of Tehran, participating in guided tours that were eye opening, showcasing the rich diversity of Iranian architecture, from ornate Qajar-era designs to contemporary buildings that punctuated the city's skyline. Each structure told a story of cultural evolution and technological advancement, narratives that I absorbed eagerly.

My confidence grew and new friendships formed were cemented

through collaborative projects and late-night study sessions. With these new friends, I explored Tehran's architectural wonders, discussing their features and historical contexts. Such discussions often extended into debates at local cafés, where we would sketch on napkins and argue over espressos about modernism versus postmodernism.

With the academic year drawing to a close, my thoughts turned towards the future. The year had not only developed my architectural skills but also broadened my horizons. Professor Baum told me I had shown 'remarkable progress' and that my designs reflected not only technical proficiency but also a 'deep understanding of the human element that is crucial in our field.'

'I owe a lot to this place, to the teachers, and to my peers,' I responded, my voice tinged with gratitude. 'But I feel like there's so much more out there to learn, to explore.'

'Indeed, the world of architecture is vast and ever evolving. Your journey has just begun,' Professor Baum replied, his eyes twinkling with encouragement. 'Consider further studies abroad, or perhaps an internship with a renowned firm. It's time to test the waters beyond these walls.'

The idea of moving abroad, to immerse myself in new cultures and architectural styles, was both thrilling and daunting. I pondered the possibilities, the cities I could visit, buildings I could learn from and diverse professionals I could work with. Little did I know how ironic those thoughts would become.

CHAPTER TEN:
PERSIAN ODYSSEY

With my elder siblings nearly 3,000 miles away in England and Switzerland, Shahin and I prepared for a Grand Tour conceived by Father. It would start with a journey to the historic city of Isfahan, the former capital of Persia. The night before our departure, the living room buzzed with anticipation. Maps were sprawled across the table. Travel guides bookmarked with notes lay beside them.

'Shahin, make sure you pack your sketchbook. Isfahan is a city of splendid vistas,' Father, reminded his youngest son.

'Yes, Baba,' Shahin replied eagerly.

I was equally enthused. 'Father, will we see the bridges and mosques I read about in school?'

'We will visit them all, my son,' Father assured, folding a map with precision. 'Isfahan was once the capital of Persia, a place of great poets and artists. You will walk the same paths as kings and scholars.'

We set off the next morning, the scenic drive to Isfahan unfolding like the pages of a vibrant history book. The landscape transitioned from the crowded streets of Tehran to serene expanses dotted with small villages and rugged mountains.

'Look at those mountains, boys,' Mother pointed out as we neared our destination. 'They say the Zayandeh River breathes life into Isfahan.'

Upon entering the city, our first stop was Nash-e Jahan Square. The immense open square, framed by the Sheikh Lotfollah Mosque and the Ali Qau Palace, was bustling with artisans and traders.

'Every tile on that mosque tells a story,' said Father, guiding us through their works. 'These are the marks of our heritage.'

As we roamed through the bazaar, I was captivated by the intricate artistry of the miniatures and handcrafted pottery. 'How can something so detailed be made by hand?' I marvelled.

'With patience and years of practice,' replied Ishmael, our guide. 'Every great achievement begins with a single, careful step.'

That evening, over dinner, the family shared their impressions …

'This city is like a poem in stone and sunlight,' Mother mused, her voice reflecting the peace she felt wandering through the historical corridors.

'Yes,' agreed Father, 'and to think, our ancestors walked here too. It's important you both understand the beauty and depth of our culture.'

On the second day of their exploration of Isfahan we visited *Menara Jonson*, an architectural marvel renowned for twin minarets resonating with each other. Climbing the narrow, spiralling stairs, Shahin and I reached the top, feeling the minarets sway in unison.

'The Swaying Minarets,' Ishmael explained, 'are a testament to Persian architectural innovation. Constructed in the fourteenth century, these twin minarets were designed to demonstrate both the might of engineering and the aesthetic sensibilities of the era. The phenomenon of one minaret swaying in response to the other being shaken is not just an architectural curiosity but a deliberate design. The minarets are interconnected through a series of beams and brackets within the structure, allowing kinetic energy to be transferred from one to the other.'

'Why do they resonate together like this?' I asked, peering curiously between the two towers.

'It's by design,' Father responded, his tone blending reverence with a hint of pride. 'Our ancestors were not just builders; but artists who played with the laws of physics to create wonders that would speak through ages.'

Transitioning between the sites during their tour in Isfahan, we marvelled at the city's seamless blend of ancient architecture and frenetic modern life, navigating intricate streets to reach the *Shaykh Bahai hammam*.

As we entered the historic monument, my curiosity was piqued. 'Father, what is this place?' I asked.

'This is a hammam,' Father explained. 'A traditional public bath, crucial to our culture for both cleanliness and relaxation.'

We moved through the elegant arches, each transition leading into warmer quarters. Father gestured towards the walls and floors. 'These are heated by a remarkable system devised by Shaykh Bahai himself. Underneath runs a network of pipes, warmed by a single candle's flame. This ingenious method distributes heat evenly throughout the hammam.'

I noticed a small flame flickering in a corner. 'Just one candle does all this?' I asked incredulously.

'Yes, exactly,' Jalil confirmed. 'It's cleverly placed as part of a larger system. The heat is amplified and spread by the building's design, a testament to the wisdom of its architect, Shaykh Bahai. He was a scholar and a visionary who used his knowledge to enhance everyday life.'

When we reached the central steam room, the heart of the hammam, the thick steam wrapped around us like a warm blanket. 'People have come to places like this for centuries not just to wash away the dust of the day, but to find a moment of peace, to enjoy the warmth in winter, and to rejuvenate their spirits,' Father continued, his voice echoing slightly off the tiled walls.

Shahin touched the damp, warm tiles curiously. 'It feels like magic,' he whispered.

'It's science and art combined,' Father said. 'Remember this place. Like the hammam's warmth that seeps slowly into your bones, let the lessons of innovation, sustainability, and tradition from our past help shape your thoughts and deeds as you grow.'

I nodded, my earlier curiosity now deepened into appreciation. 'I will, Father,' I said, a sense of understanding dawning on me as we continued their exploration.

Moving on to the Khaja Bridge, the short drive through Isfahan offered respite, allowing us to reflect on the engineering ingenuity before immersing ourselves in the bridge's lively atmosphere.

'Look at this marvel,' Father began, his voice filled with pride as they stepped onto the structure. 'The Khaja Bridge isn't merely a bridge; it's a testament to the Safavid dynasty's vision. Built in the seventeenth century by Shah Abbas II, it was both a dam and a bridge, serving multiple purposes.'

We strolled along the bridge's upper level, observing the arches spanning gracefully across the water.

'The beauty of this place lies in its details,' Father pointed out, gesturing towards the intricate tile work and paintings adorning the bridge. 'It reflects the artistic and cultural zenith of our history.'

As we walked, laughter and music drifted up from the lower levels where locals and tourists gathered to enjoy the cool breeze by the water. The atmosphere was lively, with street musicians playing traditional Persian music.

Shahin tugged at Father's sleeve, pointing towards a group of children playing near the octagonal pavilion that sat at the centre of the bridge. 'Can we go there?' he asked eagerly.

'Of course,' Father replied, leading the way. The pavilion, once used by the royal family and nobles for ceremonial purposes, now served as a favourite spot for visitors to rest and enjoy the view.

As we reached the pavilion, I leaned over the railing, watching the sun cast golden hues on the water, turning the river into a shimmering glare. 'It's like the whole bridge is alive,' I remarked, captivated by the scene.

'It's more than that,' said Father. 'This bridge is a gathering place, where art, architecture, and nature come together in harmony. It's a symbol of connection – not just between two banks of a river, but between people, between past and present.'

We spent the afternoon at the bridge, immersing ourselves in the social scene, sharing stories with locals, and learning more about the bridge's history.

At a nearby café, we reflected on our visit. 'Each visit to places like Khaja Bridge,' Father mused, 'strengthens our bonds with our heritage, teaching us the value of beauty and the importance of preserving it for future generations.'

I nodded, my mind full of images and stories from the day. 'I think I understand now why you love these journeys so much,' I told Father. 'They're not just trips. They're lessons in living, in appreciating what we have and striving to protect it.'

Father smiled, his eyes twinkling with satisfaction. 'Exactly. As you grow, you'll carry these lessons with you, shaping how you see the world and your place in it.'

The next day, as we wandered deeper into the heart of Isfahan's thronging bazaars, the hum of commerce and culture grew louder. The air was rich with the scents of spices and freshly baked bread, mingling with the more delicate fragrances of rosewater and saffron emanating from nearby stalls. I was drawn to a vendor showcasing exquisite Persian miniatures, each detailed painting a story of epic battles and poetic love. The vendor launched into tales of each miniature's origin, weaving historical facts with folklore, his voice rising and falling with the rhythm of a seasoned storyteller.

Meanwhile, Shahin found himself mesmerised by a potter at his wheel, the clay dancing between the craftsman's skilled hands. The potter explained the significance of the designs, each pattern representing different elements of Persian life: the peacock for divinity, the cypress tree for eternal life. As he spoke, Shahin's eyes followed the smooth movements that converted the earthy lump into a pot of elegant proportions.

Father was deep in conversation with a fabric merchant, discussing the techniques used in weaving Persian rugs. The merchant unfurled a particularly stunning carpet to demonstrate the vibrant dyes made from natural ingredients found in the Persian landscape. 'Each rug,' he proclaimed, 'carries the soul of the weaver and the spirit of our land.'

Father then led his family to a quieter section of the bazaar, where a small workshop tucked away behind the main thoroughfare revealed artisans at work on metal engraving. The metallic taps of hammers on copper filled the air as intricate designs emerged under the hands of the master craftsman. He shared the symbolism behind the motifs, pointing out elements that promised prosperity and health to any home the piece graced.

As the afternoon waned, we paused at a café draped in hanging vines, savouring cups of thick, aromatic Persian tea. Around us locals gathered, their voices a blend of earnest debate and hearty laughter. The bazaar was more than a place of trade: it was the beating heart of Isfahan, pulsing with the lifeblood of its people.

Refreshed, we continued our exploration, coming across a calligrapher who expertly brushed strokes of elegant script onto aged parchment. He invited us to try the ancient art, guiding us as we attempted to mimic the fluid movements required to produce each character.

As evening approached, we found ourselves in a square where musicians gathered to play traditional Persian instruments. The haunting melodies of the *tar* and *Santoor* blended beautifully with the deeper tones of the *daft*, creating a soundtrack that seemed to wrap the setting sun in a warm embrace.

The day concluded with a light meal at a nearby restaurant, where the conversations returned to the wonders we had seen. Father expressed his hope that the experiences would enrich his sons' understanding of their heritage. 'These traditions,' he mused, 'are what bind us to our past and guide us to our future.'

As we concluded our journey through Isfahan, I felt a profound connection to my Persian heritage.

'The beauty of these places isn't just in their stones and tiles,' I said, 'but in the stories they tell us. Stories of innovation, art, and community that have survived through centuries.'

Father nodded in agreement, his eyes reflecting a similar spark of pride. 'Yes. These stories are now a part of you, just as they were once a part of your ancestors,' he replied

'This journey,' I said, 'has shown me the true essence of our culture. It's a living, breathing heritage that I'm proud to inherit and pass on. Isfahan isn't just a city of the past; it's a beacon for the future.'

SHIRAZ, CITY OF POETS AND ROSES

Next, we set our sights on Shiraz, the city of poets and roses. As our car wound through the rugged landscapes separating these historical jewels, the anticipation in the air was palpable. Sitting by the window, I watched the scenery transition from stark mountain faces to more gentle, verdant slopes as we approached Shiraz.

'Shiraz has a different spirit, a soul crafted by poets and kings,' Father explained. 'It's a city that sings to the hearts of those who walk its streets. Shiraz is not just about its past but how beautifully it blends with the present.'

Entering Shiraz, the air seemed to shift. There was a sweetness to it, laden with the scent of blossoming flowers from the many gardens that defined the city. It was a stark contrast to Isfahan's grandeur, offering a softer, more introspective beauty.

'Every corner of this city has a verse attached to it, a line of poetry that echoes through the ages,' remarked Father as we strolled through the Eram Garden, a burst of colour and fragrance, with pathways lined by towering cypress trees and an array of floral spectacles dazzling the senses.

'The poets of Shiraz didn't just write,' I observed. 'They were inspired, they lived their verses.'

'Yes,' affirmed Father. 'And it's said that the beauty of Shiraz would turn any sceptic into a poet.'

As the day faded, we found ourselves at the tomb of the poet Hafez. The atmosphere was serene, almost sacred, with visitors whispering verses as they meandered through the memorial. I listened intently as a local recited a ghazal, the lyrical quality of the verse blending seamlessly with the rustling of the leaves above.

'This is why Shiraz is special,' Mother said softly, her words almost a whisper. 'It's where poetry is the very breath of the city.'

Next morning, Shiraz unfurled its charms as we wandered along its storied boulevards. The city was alive with the chatter of café-goers and the aromatic scents of freshly brewed coffee and sweet sharbat. We were captivated by the blend of modern vibrancy and timeless tradition.

'The poets who walked these streets left their mark not just in books, but in the very spirit of the city,' Father explained. The site was a serene enclave where the air seemed thick with literary history. Visitors moved quietly among the rose gardens that flanked the poet's resting place, their faces reflective and reverent.

'Listen to the verses,' Mother whispered, pointing to a group of students reciting Hafez's ghazals. The lyrical sounds, almost musical, resonated within the marble halls and among the flowering paths, infusing the space with a sense of continuity between past and present.

Next stop was the tomb of Saadi, another luminary of Persian literature. Here, the connection between Shiraz's cultural heritage and its current identity was even more palpable. Saadi's words, part of a larger work, are inscribed on the entrance, welcoming all who came: 'Human beings are members of a whole, in creation of one essence and soul.'

As we wandered through the interconnected gardens and mausoleums, I felt inspired by the enduring wisdom of these poets. 'They wrote about life, love, and unity,' I noted. 'It's like they still speak to us, guiding through their words.'

The path then led to the Arg of Karim Khan, an imposing citadel at the city centre. The walls, robust and weathered, told tales of historical sieges and royal residencies. As we toured the interior, transformed into a museum, we admired the blend of military architecture and residential elegance.

Later, we strolled through the Vakil Bazaar, a lively marketplace that offered everything from exquisite Persian carpets to handcrafted silverware. The bazaar was a labyrinth of alleys and shops, each turn revealing new scents and sounds. Here we interacted with local artisans, with Shahin and I trying miniature painting, a traditional Persian art form. 'Each brushstroke tells a story,' we were told, as an artist guided our hands.

As evening approached, we visited the Nasir al-Mulk Mosque, also known as the Pink Mosque. The setting sun ignited the stained-glass windows, bathing the interior in a kaleidoscope of light. 'It's like stepping inside a jewel,' Mother whispered.

PERSEPOLIS, CAPITAL OF THE ACHAEMENID EMPIRE

Persepolis in Iran

The final leg of our adventure was the journey from vibrant Shiraz to the solemn quietude of the ancient ruins of Persepolis, the ancient capital of the Achaemenid Empire, founded in 518 BCE, many years before the current era. The drive, winding through landscapes that blended harsh desert terrains with occasional bursts of lush greenery.

As they arrived, the sheer scale of Persepolis unfolded before them. The towering columns, majestic staircases, and expansive courtyards spoke of an era where it stood as the ceremonial capital of the Persian Empire. 'Imagine the grandeur of the celebrations held here,' Jalil said, gesturing towards the ruins that sprawled out like the bones of a forgotten world.

We began our tour at the Gate of All Nations, greeted by the imposing figures of *lamassus* – winged bulls with the heads of bearded men, meant to guard the empire. Our guide, a knowledgeable local historian, recounted tales of kings and conquerors, lavish feasts and grand assemblies. With each story, the ruins of Persepolis came alive, whispering secrets of ancient ceremonies and the echoes of a powerful civilisation that once commanded vast territories.

As we moved towards the Apadana, the great audience hall, I could almost hear the clatter of soldiers and the murmur of courtiers that might have filled the air. The guide pointed out the intricate bas-reliefs that lined the staircases, depicting scenes of tribute bearers from the many corners of the empire. 'These images,' he explained, 'represent the diversity and vastness of the Achaemenid Empire, showcasing figures from as far as India and Ethiopia bringing gifts for the king.'

The history lesson was immersive, the visual splendour of the ruins blending seamlessly with the narrative. Sketchbook in hand, I tried to capture the essence of the reliefs, my lines tracing the history etched in stone.

As we ventured deeper into Persepolis, we approached the treasury and the Hundred Columns Hall, areas less frequented by the casual tourist, yet rich with history. The air seemed charged with the ancient mysteries held within the stone walls. I listened intently as our guide described how these structures functioned not just as physical entities but as symbols of the empire's power and wealth.

'The treasury,' he began, 'was more than a storehouse. It was a statement of the wealth that flowed through Persepolis, a testament to the empire's reach across continents.' He pointed out the remains of stone doorways, their thresholds worn down by the passage of countless treasures. I imagined caravans arriving laden with gold, silver, and precious stones, the treasures of a world empire. Moving on to the Hundred Columns Hall, the guide explained its use as a grand reception hall by King Darius. 'This was where the king displayed his splendour to visiting dignitaries,' he said, gesturing to the still-standing columns that seemed to defy time. 'Each column here,' he noted, 'was once topped with elaborate capitals, likely made of precious metals and stones, though now lost to history.'

As we walked through the hall, Mother, moved by the beauty of the ruins, said it was 'like walking through a painting, each step a brushstroke of history.' Her words resonated with the family, each member feeling the weight of history surrounding them.

The guide led us to an overlook offering a panoramic view of the site. The strategic layout of Persepolis was evident, with its ceremonial and administrative sections clearly delineated. 'Persepolis was designed to impress but also to function,' he said. 'The precision of its urban planning is a reflection of the Achaemenid administration's sophistication.'

As the shadows lengthened, the guide shared tales of the annual *Norouz* festival, when representatives from all the provinces brought their tributes to the king. 'Imagine this place, filled with people from all over the empire, celebrating the new year with feasts and music,' he mused.

Our exploration concluded at the tombs of King Darius and his successors, carved into a nearby cliff, with the guide speaking of the continuity and legacy of leadership. 'It wasn't just stone and inscriptions: it was a message across time.'

As the day waned into a soft twilight, we found ourselves seated near the grand staircase of Persepolis, where once ancient monarchs might have addressed their subjects. The guide delved into the philosophical implications of Persepolis' legacy.

'Consider this,' he began. 'The builders of Persepolis not only created a capital but also a statement of cultural identity that has transcended centuries.'

'Do you think they knew the impact they would have on history?' I asked.

The guide nodded thoughtfully. 'It's likely they hoped to immortalise their civilisation's achievements. Every column, every statue here was designed to convey a message of power and enlightenment to both their contemporaries and future generations.'

Intricate bas-reliefs depicting scenes of royal audiences and ceremonial offerings, the guide explained, were not mere decorations but visual narratives intended to communicate the empire's prowess and piety to all who walked these grounds.

Taking a final look at the grandeur of Persepolis under the stars, our guide's parting words resonated deeply: 'Just as we learn from these ruins, what we build and the stories we tell will inform future generations about our time and what was important to us.'

As our car wound its way back to Tehran, I was deep in thought. The journey to Isfahan and Shiraz, capped by the profound visit to Persepolis, had left an indelible mark on my young mind.

Traditional Iranian bakery

CHAPTER ELEVEN:
TIME TO LEAVE

My elder siblings' first encounter with London in the late 1960s was a sensory overload, as they stepped into a world vastly different from the warm, familiar streets of Tehran. The chill of the English air was a sharp contrast to the dry heat they were accustomed to, and even the sunlight seemed muted beneath the persistent grey clouds.

As they navigated through the crowds at Heathrow Airport, the cacophony of a new language made their heads spin. Everything moved faster, people striding with purpose, and relentless traffic on the left side of the road adding to their disorientation.

Carnaby Street vibrated with rock music, a kaleidoscope of psychedelic prints and miniskirts, with impromptu gatherings of free-spirited youths discussing art, politics, and freedom – a stark contrast to the reserved ambience of Tehran.

Their first meal, classic English fish and chips, was a far cry from the rich, aromatic flavours of Persian cuisine. Although perfectly fried, the fish lacked the spices they loved. The chips, though hearty, were too bland without a dusting of saffron or turmeric. Their taste buds struggled to adapt to the simplicity of salt and vinegar.

They marvelled at the quaint architecture, the centuries-old buildings mingling with modern facades, and the sprawling parks that offered a splash of green amid the urban expanse. Yet, each sight and sound also sharpened the pang of missing home – the calls to prayer, bustling bazaars and the warmth of direct sunlight, a rare commodity in London.

Living with the Jalili family softened the edge of their cultural shock. Mr Jalili, with his connections to the Persian consulate, provided a comforting link to their homeland, while his anecdotes of life in the UK bridged the gap between the familiar and the foreign. His wife, a gracious host, tried to introduce them to British customs and cuisine.

Evenings were spent with young Omid Jalili – now a well-known comedian. His playful antics brought laughter and lightness into their adjustment period. Watching him mimic television characters or recount his adventures at school, Massoud, Hedi, and Nadereh found joy in the universal language of laughter, which helped knit the fabric of their new life in this strange, bustling city.

As they lay in bed each night, listening to the unfamiliar sounds of the city, they whispered to each other in Farsi, recounting the day's experiences and making plans for the next. Each conversation was a step towards building a bridge between their past in Tehran and their future in England.

The Jalili household was in a quaint London suburb, close to a 'tube' station and bus stop providing easy access to central London. The narrow house, with dark grey bricks from a century of pollution, stood silent at the end of a long road of identical residences. A brightly painted front door with climbing roses over the entrance set it apart.

This was a sanctuary for Massoud, Hedi, and Nadereh as they navigated their initial days in England. Mr Jalili, a seasoned photographer at the Persian consulate, brought a comforting sense of familiarity to their strange new environment. His stories of diplomatic events and cultural nuances of life in London were enlightening and reassuring.

Each evening, they gathered around the Jalili's dining table, where discussions ranged from politics to Persian poetry, blending the old with the new. Mrs Jalili, with her keen sense of hospitality, introduced them to English customs and tea-time etiquette, often punctuated by the cheerful interruptions of young Omid, whose youthful exuberance added joy to their adjustment.

'Remember, you're not just here to study, but to absorb, to learn from everything around you,' Mr Jalili would say, as he encouraged them to explore beyond the academic world. His insights into the cultural diversity of London helped bridge the gap between their Iranian heritage and new British surroundings.

Omid was a constant reminder of the innocence and adaptability of youth. His imaginative play and endless questions about Iran sparked conversations that reminded them of home, yet encouraged them to embrace their new setting. 'Why do you speak so funny?' Omid would ask, his head cocked to one side, sparking laughter and leading to impromptu Farsi lessons in the living room.

Each weekend, Mr Jalili would take them to community gatherings and events at the consulate, providing them with a broader perspective of the Iranian diaspora's role in London and helping build a network of friends and mentors to support them throughout their stay.

Mrs Jalili taught Nadereh to knit and navigate the local markets. 'It's like weaving a new pattern into your life,' Mrs Jalili would say as they knitted. 'Each stitch represents a challenge you've met, a lesson you've learned.'

As the seasons changed, so did the siblings' perception of London, the initial shock of the cold weather gradually giving way to an appreciation of the crisp autumn leaves and the occasional sunny day.

Their stay with the Jalilis laid a strong foundation for their years in England. In this nurturing environment, they began to blend the vibrant colours of their Iranian roots with the subtle hues of their British experiences, enrolling at a language school, visiting their local pub and learning to say: 'Three beers please.'

One day, after struggling with a particularly challenging pronunciation lesson, Hedi leaned over to Massoud with a wry smile. 'Can you believe it? We came all this way to twist our tongues into knots!'

Massoud chuckled but kept his eyes on his notebook. 'It's like our tongues need to be as flexible as gymnasts to get these sounds right. But we'll manage, you'll see.'

In one of their practice sessions, their classmate Emily noticed their difficulties. She approached with a friendly grin. 'Need some help with those tricky diphthongs?' she offered.

Nadereh welcomed the offer. 'Yes, please, Emily. I think we're losing a battle with English here.'

Emily laughed, pulling up a chair. 'Don't worry, everyone struggles at first. Think of "th" as the soft brushing of your tongue against your front teeth.' She demonstrated, and they mimicked her, gradually getting better with each attempt.

As they ventured into the city, they practiced their English relentlessly, ordering food, asking for directions or simply engaging with shopkeepers. They began to appreciate the nuances of English more, and with each day, the language felt less foreign.

Reflecting on these challenges later, Nadereh wrote in her journal, 'Every conversation, every mistake, and every correction is a step closer to fluency. We are not just learning a language; we are embracing a new way of life.'

However, the time came when the three oldest siblings had to leave the Jalili household. Father had meticulously arranged their next steps in education, which involved geographical separations but promised greater opportunities. Nadereh was to return to Tehran for a brief period before embarking to Geneva for advanced studies, while Massoud and Hedi were bound for boarding school in Sussex.

First to leave was Nadereh. She shared fond farewells, first with Massoud and Hedi and then with the Jalili family before disappearing into immigration at Heathrow Airport. On the day of her flight to Geneva, the family drove her to the airport. The goodbye was heartfelt. Father embraced his daughter tightly. 'Remember, you're not just learning for yourself, but to bring that knowledge back home someday.'

Not long after that Massoud and Hedi waved goodbye to 1960's London, travelling to the stately architecture of their new boarding school, whose strict schedule and disciplined environment was in stark contrast to the relaxed atmosphere at the Jalili household.

Days began with morning bell at dawn, followed by classes that were challenging and invigorating. Hedi found the mathematics and science courses demanding but was quickly fascinated by the depth of knowledge his teachers brought into the classroom.

Massoud showed a keen interest in literature and history, subjects that allowed him to draw connections between his Persian heritage and the Western narratives he was being taught.

The brothers often spent their evenings discussing these new ideas and debating their implications. Gradually, they became fixtures in the school's debate club, where they honed their skills in rhetoric and critical thinking.

Sports played a significant part in their daily lives. The school's emphasis on physical education meant that afternoons were spent on the rugby or soccer field or the tennis courts. Here, Hedi and Massoud not only built their physical strength but also learned the value of teamwork and leadership – qualities that were encouraged and celebrated.

'The discipline here is something else,' Massoud confided to Hedi one crisp autumn evening as they walked back to their dormitory after a strenuous day of academics and athletics. 'But I feel like it's moulding us into well-rounded individuals.'

Hedi nodded in agreement, his breath visible in the cool air. 'It's tough, but I guess that's what it takes to excel. I miss home, but there's something about this place that feels right.'

The initial homesickness, the struggle to keep up with native English speakers, and the cold weather were constant reminders of how far they were from Tehran. However, as months turned into years, the brothers carved out a space for themselves, respected by peers and teachers alike for their perseverance and unique perspectives.

At weekends, the school often arranged trips to historical sites across England, providing the brothers with a broader understanding of the country's heritage. These outings were not just educational but also a source of inspiration for both, as they connected the dots between the lessons in class and the real world.

As their time at the boarding school progressed, Massoud and Hedi grew into confident young men, ready to face the complexities of the world with a balanced view shaped by both their Iranian upbringing and their education in England. Their integration into British culture had been gradual but profound. Beyond the confines of their boarding school, they began to explore local traditions and partake in cultural events that were initially foreign to them. As the seasons changed, they experienced their first Guy Fawkes night, where fireworks lit up the autumn sky. They stood among their classmates, learning the historical significance of the event, which sparked discussions about the differences between British and Persian historical celebrations.

'It's fascinating how history is remembered and celebrated so vividly here,' Hedi remarked as a rocket exploded in a burst of colour overhead.

'Yes, and each of these traditions tells a story, much like our own Nowruz or Yalda Night back home,' Massoud replied, drawing parallels that helped bridge their old and new worlds.

Not long after this, they attended a traditional British Christmas celebration. The school hosted a grand dinner, complete with a choir singing carols and a beautifully decorated Christmas tree. For the brothers, who had never experienced anything quite like it back in Tehran, the warmth and communal spirit of the celebration were deeply touching.

'Look at this, Hedi,' Massoud whispered during the choir's performance. 'It's so different from our celebrations, but there's a similar sense of community and joy.'

Hedi nodded, his eyes reflecting the soft glow of the Christmas lights. 'It's beautiful. I never imagined we'd be part of something like this.'

In the spring, they played cricket, and ventured to a local match, the sport entirely new to them. Watching the game and understanding its rules became a weekend activity. Gradually, they not only appreciated the sport but also participated in school matches, learning teamwork and strategy in a context very different from any they had known. Through these experiences, Massoud and Hedi's understanding of and appreciation for British culture deepened.

My transition, meanwhile, was just about to begin. On a bright Sunday afternoon in the late 1960s, I was called into Father's study. Being summoned like this usually foretold some major event, good or bad. He was standing by the window, his posture unusually rigid, hinting at the gravity of the conversation to follow.

'We need to talk about your future,' he began, turning to face me. Mother was already seated, her expression sombre yet encouraging. Sensing the seriousness, I sat upright, attentive.

'Your mother and I have made a decision. It's time for you to broaden your horizons, to see more of the world and to learn from it,' Father continued.

I felt a flutter of nerves. 'Are you sending me to England?' I asked.

'Yes, but not directly,' Father replied. 'First, you will spend three months in Geneva with Nadereh. It's a chance for you to adjust to living abroad before you move on to England.' The mixture of excitement and apprehension was palpable. Geneva, a place so distant and different, was to be my first step into the unknown. 'Why Geneva?' I inquired, curiosity threading through my initial shock.

'Your sister has settled there well, and it will be good for you to have a familiar face help you transition,' Mother explained, her tone reassuring. 'This will prepare you for your studies in England.'

I nodded, processing the layers of this unexpected plan. The idea of living abroad was thrilling but daunting. 'When do I leave?' I finally asked.

'In a few weeks. We have a lot to prepare, and I want you to be fully ready for this journey,' said Father.

I felt a deep, stirring mix of anticipation and nostalgia, aware that I was on the brink of a profound new chapter. The journey wasn't just a physical move from Tehran to Geneva but a passage into new realms of personal growth and understanding.

The weeks that followed were a flurry of activity, getting travel documents, packing and preparing for my new life. The preparation wasn't just about logistics; it was also about ensuring I felt ready emotionally and mentally. Family evenings were filled with discussions about Swiss culture, the importance of being open to new experiences, and how to deal with homesickness.

One evening, as I packed Shahin came into my room, a slight tremble in his voice. 'Are you going to forget about us when you're all famous and studying abroad?' he half-joked. I put down a stack of books and pulled my brother into a hug.

'Never could I ever forget you. You'll have to write to me about everything, promise?'

'Promise.' He nodded.

The night before my departure, the family gathered around the dinner table for a farewell feast. It was an emotional meal, filled with laughter and tears, as all shared their favourite memories and hopes for my future.

When the morning of my departure arrived, the Hashtroudi home stood in darkness as the family loaded the last of my luggage into the car for the early morning flight. Father was behind the wheel, while Mother fussed over me.

'Every great journey begins with a single step, or in your case, a plane ride,' said Father.

I managed a small smile, appreciating my father's effort. 'I just wish this first step wasn't so far from home.'

Mother reached over from the back seat to squeeze my shoulder. 'Home is not just a place. It's where your family is, and we are always with you in your heart.'

Pulling up to the departure area, they unloaded my luggage, and the reality of the goodbye settled over us like a heavy blanket. 'Be curious, learn much, and come back a man who can change the world,' Father said as he embraced me.

Mother, her eyes brimming with tears, held me a little longer. 'And no matter how far you go, remember, there's a light always on for you at home.'

As I walked through the security gate, I turned back for one last look. I boarded the Douglas DC-8, my heart pounding with the thrill of my first flight. As I stepped inside, I was greeted by a cabin exuding a sense of the era's optimism and technological prowess. It was my first time flying, and I travelled alone on the Swissair flight. At the airport, my mother, concerned for my safety, asked if one of the flight attendants could look after me. A kind woman called Miss Thompson took me under her wing, making sure I was comfortable during the flight.

The excitement built as the engines roared to life, sending a thrilling vibration through the cabin. I pressed my face against the window, watching as the ground crew waved their final signals before the plane began its taxi to the runway.

As the plane ascended, the landscape of Iran unfolded beneath me. To the south, the sprawling oil fields of Khuzestan were visible, their gas flares piercing through the dull early morning light like flickering beacons against the dusky terrain. The patchwork of rugged mountains and arid plains rolled away beneath the wings, each fold of the earth telling stories of ancient civilisations. Perhaps, if the flight path favoured it, the ruins of Persepolis might glimpse up, their time-worn stones a testament to the grandeur of bygone eras. As the plane climbed higher, the chaotic beauty of Tehran's expanding cityscape faded into the haze, giving way to the stark, serene expanses of the Iranian plateau.

When the captain announced the beginning of their descent into Geneva, I felt both sadness and anticipation. The flight had been a profound journey, not just across the globe but into new realms of understanding and possibility.

The aircraft's wheels touched down heavily, and the descent seemed endless. I peered out of the window, absorbing my first view of Geneva – a city that promised new adventures and learning.

Inside the terminal, I followed the herd through the sleek corridors, my heart racing with anticipation, my eyes scanning the crowd until they landed on a familiar face: Nadereh, waiting with an open smile.

'Shab,' she exclaimed, her arms open for a hug that bridged the gap of years and miles. 'Look at you, all grown up!'

'I can't believe I'm actually here,' I replied, returning her embrace.

As we walked to the car, Nadereh pointed out landmarks, and I listened intently, my mind trying to capture every detail. The drive from the airport was a blur of new sights; the clean, orderly streets of Geneva were lined with elegant buildings and lush parks, so different from the chaotic beauty of Tehran.

Sitting beside Nadereh, I reflected on my journey. 'It's so much to take in,' I confessed. 'Leaving home, flying alone … It's all been a huge leap.'

Nadereh nodded, her expression understanding. 'It's the first of many leaps. Each one will teach you something valuable. This is just the beginning of your story.'

As we crossed Lake Geneva, the setting sun cast a golden glow over the water, and I felt a profound sense of transition. This was no longer just a visit; it was the start of something new, a period of growth and exploration.

'I'm excited and scared all at once,' I admitted, watching the water sparkle beneath the last rays of sunlight.

'That's perfectly normal,' Nadereh reassured me. 'Use that feeling, learn from it. You're not just here to study architecture; you're here to build the foundations of your future.'

The car turned into the driveway of Nadereh's apartment, marking the end of our journey from the airport but the beginning of my new life phase. As I unpacked my bags that evening, I thought about my parents, my little brother Shahin, my home, and the path ahead.

'This journey isn't just about leaving home,' I mused, looking out at the night lights of Geneva. 'It's about discovering who I am apart from my family, my country. It's about seeing what I can become.'

Little did I know it at the time but these few months in Geneva, and my later time in the United Kingdom, were to be major chapters not merely in my education but in the very fabric of my life.

PART THREE: BUILDING A BUSINESS AND LIFE

CHAPTER TWELVE:
END OF AN ERA

In Geneva, I was immediately immersed in a new world. Everyone around me spoke French, and Nadereh's friends spoke both French and English. I communicated in English, as my French was still quite rudimentary. I had always struggled with languages, and my German was no better. I could understand more than I could speak, but it wasn't enough to have fluent conversations.

My time in Switzerland was brief, but unforgettable. I remember the beautiful fountains on Geneva Lake, the lovely restaurants, and the breathtaking mountains surrounding the city.

Sometimes, I would wait for my sister at the Mövenpick restaurant sitting by the bar. The bartender got to know me, and we'd communicate in my broken English, with a few French words sprinkled in.

Nadereh introduced me to Swiss culture, which I grew to love. We went trekking in the mountains, and I was mesmerised by the stunning views. Ironically, many years later, when I married Gaby, I discovered that she was originally from Lausanne, a town near

Geneva that I had visited many times with Nadereh. Gaby, who had moved to Zürich at the age of nine due to her father's job, took me back to the mountains there to teach me how to ski.

I always felt a deep connection to Switzerland – the mountains, people, and food. I loved the trams running through the towns powered entirely by electricity, an advanced feature back then. It was winter when I first arrived and Geneva looked magical blanketed in snow. I recall shopping with my sister in a supermarket called Migros, which boasted the best meat and fish counters a fantastic array of fruit and vegetables. I also enjoyed visiting a boutique around the corner from my sister's house, where I bought clothes with money my father had sent me.

We took a trip to Chamonix, enjoying the cable car ride and the scenic train journey, rode a boat on Lake Geneva, soaking in the mountain views, and drove to Mont Blanc, passing through a long tunnel to reach the glacier at 3,000 feet. It was an awe-inspiring sight.

Nadereh was working at an American company located just across the border in France. Each morning, she would take a bus to work, returning every evening. I admired her independence and dedication. She lived in a shared house with five girls from different backgrounds, creating a lively and multicultural environment. There was her close friend Lili, a stunningly beautiful Persian, Swiss-German Ruth, Lamis from Turkey, and Lebis and Lea, two sisters from Vietnam. I basked in attention from the girls. Being the youngest and the only boy in the house, I was spoiled with care. Whether it was coffee, dinner, or just a walk around the city, one or two of the girls would often take me out. I was rarely alone, and absolutely loved it. It was an exciting and memorable time.

After two months, my parents decided it was time for me to join my brothers in Bournemouth. Leaving Geneva was bittersweet, but I looked forward to reuniting with Massoud and Hedi. Upon landing at Heathrow Airport, I was greeted by my brothers. I'll never forget that moment – Massoud looked sharp and well-dressed as always, while Hedi had grown a full Afro, resembling Jimi Hendrix. At first, I didn't recognise him! It was only after a moment of surprise that I realised who he was.

Massoud drove us back to Bournemouth in his Ford Anglia, a two-hour journey filled with chatter and laughter. When we arrived, I was introduced to our new home – a spacious flat near the beach that we shared with other Iranian boys. The flat was beautiful, and being so close to the sea made it even more special.

Life in Bournemouth was vibrant. Massoud and Hedi spent their mornings at college, evenings studying and weekends invariably at a local club. For me, the routine began with enrolling in a language school in Bournemouth, where I studied English. We moved to a larger house divided into two flats. My brothers and I took the ground-floor flat, while the upper flat was occupied by two British law students: David Ellis and Desmond Layton. Over time, we became close friends. Both were kind and full of life, and we spent many happy times together. Years later, they became our trusted lawyers, helping us navigate commercial matters. David sadly passed away a few years ago, while Desmond has retired. I'll always treasure the memories we shared.

At Bournemouth College, Massoud met Jacqueline, a Swiss girl with striking blue eyes, and white-blond hair who stood at about 5ft 2ins – a similar height to him. They fell in love and made an adorable couple, really suiting each other. She moved in with us and we all lived together until Hedi later went to Plymouth to study interior design.

After I moved to study at Salisbury College, Massoud and Jacqueline relocated to Geneva, where Jacqueline became very close friends with Nadereh. As Nadereh received a job offer in Paris, moving there to start a new chapter of her life, Jacqueline began working for Swissair at Geneva airport. Her job allowed her to travel the world and she could bring a companion along, which benefited Massoud greatly. They travelled frequently and one of their favourite destinations was Hawaii.

Massoud managed to enrol me at the University of Hawaii to study architecture, which had always been my passion and a natural progression from my studies at a technical college in Tehran. Massoud also enrolled himself at another institution in Hawaii. I was beyond excited. I had never been to Hawaii, but had seen pictures, brochures, and heard so much about the beautiful beaches and surf. I couldn't wait to get there.

Massoud planned to fly to the UK to join me, and Jacqueline would follow later. I was over the moon, knowing we'd all be going to Hawaii together. However, after just a few days, everything changed. The phone rang in a flat I was sharing with friends, and it was Massoud. He told me to sit down, and I immediately thought he was joking. But the news was devastating: my dear father, at the age of forty-eight, had suffered a heart attack and passed away. Massoud had received the news from my mother.

I was absolutely traumatised and Massoud insisted that I stay put while he caught the first flight to the UK. For days, I didn't leave my flat or eat. Grief overwhelmed me.

CHAPTER THIRTEEN:
BEHIND DIFFERENT BARS

After Massoud arrived, we tried to comfort each other, though both of us were struggling. We called my mother many times, asking her to arrange tickets so we could return to Tehran, but she advised us to stay where we were. If we had returned, we would have been required to serve our two-year military service, compulsory for boys over eighteen.

I stopped going to college, while Massoud stayed on a tourist visa. Our options were limited; we had to either return to college or go back to Tehran. So, we decided to move to London while we sorted things out. In London, I found a job in a boutique called Bugatti and we took a flat together behind King's Road in Chelsea. Each evening after work, we'd meet up at a bar called Blushes.

Our visa situation was becoming urgent, and we were getting desperate. A friend suggested that if we enrolled in a hairdressing school, which was inexpensive, we could get a visa. We took the advice and were soon enrolled at a hairdressing school, which was later taken over by Vidal Sassoon. Surprisingly, we both excelled at it and enjoyed the training. We found work as hairdressers, and it turned out to be a fulfilling and lucrative job.

Two years had passed since my father's death, and Mother still didn't want us to return. She managed to retain some assets, but most of my father's wealth was taken by his brothers, which was devastating for her, as she had never been involved in his business affairs.

On some weekends, we would go to visit friends in Bournemouth and on one trip a Persian man we didn't know well introduced us to a mutual friend who offered to sell us his coffee shop. We returned to London, called Mother and explained that buying the outlet would give us an income and allow us to apply for a work visa to stay in the UK. After long discussions, she agreed and sent us £13,000.

Caesars Coffee Shop was the beginning of a new chapter for us. For the first time, we had to manage our finances and look after ourselves without Father's support. It was a challenging but formative time in our lives and we grew up quickly.

THE BIRTH OF ALCATRAZ

On May 24, 1974, Massoud and I found ourselves sitting in David Ellis's office with Desmond Leyden. The air was thick with anticipation as we signed the papers for the Caesars purchase. With a final handshake, the keys were handed over. We were brimming with excitement, though we knew little about the workings of a business, let alone running a coffee shop.

Bournemouth was bustling with the May Bank Holiday crowds, making it an ideal time to take over. However, the first night did not go as smoothly as we had imagined. A major fight broke out between two groups of customers. It escalated quickly, and we had to call the police, close the doors and clear the place. The experience was overwhelming, but we were determined not to let it get to us. We quickly found a solution, hiring one of the boys as a doorman to keep order. It was our first taste of how chaotic things could get, but we were in it for the long haul. There was no backing down.

Caesars operated from 9am to 3am, seven days a week, and we rarely took a day off. We were young, eager, and willing to work hard. But as we began to settle into the routine, we realised there was potential for more. The coffee shop's basement had been partially converted into a restaurant by the previous owner but resembled a prison corridor, with vertical metal bars running from the back of the benches to the ceiling. It looked a bit intimidating but we saw an opportunity.

We envisioned an American-style burger restaurant, a concept beginning to gain popularity in the UK. Two famous eateries, *'American Success'* and *'American Disaster'* had made waves in London and we thought we could bring that vibe to the south coast. We decided to call it *Alcatraz*, capturing the essence of the space's industrial feel.

The transformation of the basement took several months. We left the metal bars intact, paying homage to the prison-like atmosphere, which gave the restaurant its signature style. The décor was inspired by the iconic scenes from *The Godfather* movie, bringing a touch of Hollywood to the south coast. We hired two Malaysian students, Eddie Tong and Lee Chang, both studying catering at Bournemouth University, where they would later go on to teach catering and tourism.

We created a simple menu with items that would stand out, giving each item a unique name that tied into the restaurant's theme:

- *Straight ATE* – A plain burger
- *Racketeer* – burger with barbecue sauce
- *Antisocial* – burger with garlic butter
- *Convertible* – burger topped with egg sunny-side-up
- *Incognito* – burger with melted cheese
- *Hunger Strike* – burger with no bun and salad
- *Bugsy Malone* – roast half-chicken
- *Al Capone* – fillet steak

We served one type of beer and red and white wine, all branded *Alcatraz*. The simplicity of the menu and the quality of the food made the restaurant an instant hit. Every evening, there was a queue outside and we had no reservations policy – first come, first served. The music was always on point. I would travel to London to pick up the latest albums, ensuring that our playlist stood out. DJs from nearby nightclubs even came to check out our music.

Massoud ran *Caesars*, while I took charge of *Alcatraz American Restaurant*. After a year, we expanded further, purchasing the shop next door and relocating the American restaurant there, while converting the whole of the existing site into *Alcatraz Nightclub*.

A NIGHTCLUB AND A LICENCE

With the new nightclub came new challenges. We applied for a private club licence, which would allow us to operate the venue legally. The hearing was set at the magistrate's court, where Massoud, David Ellis, and I appeared before the magistrates. They informed me that I was the youngest person in history to have been granted a private club licence by this court, a moment that filled me with both pride and responsibility.

I promised the court that we would obey the law and ensure the club ran smoothly. *Alcatraz* was now officially a nightclub. Caesars was a thing of the past, and the new *Alcatraz American Burgers* had been born. The nightclub quickly became a staple on Bournemouth's nightlife scene, hosting special events, including tribute nights to famous DJs. One of the most memorable nights came when I discovered a Michael Jackson tribute act in London. I was so impressed that I immediately hired him for a trial performance. The night was a resounding success and when we booked him again, the line to get in was stretched around the block.

During that second performance, the police arrived. Massoud called me outside, concerned about the large crowd. I explained that we had a performer and, as long as we maintained security, we were in control. They gave us the green light, and the show continued without a hitch.

For the grand finale of the night, we used a smoke machine to create a dramatic atmosphere on the dance floor. Four security guards would carry a wooden coffin down the stairs and as the music from *Thriller* began to play, the coffin lid would open and the Michael Jackson lookalike would emerge, performing the famous dance moves. The crowd went wild, and word quickly spread about the spectacle. People travelled from surrounding towns just to witness the show.

Back in Tehran, Shahin was about to join us. My mother had told me she was sending him to the UK to continue his education. I began looking for a suitable boarding school, but none felt right so I decided to enrol him in a language school, where he could study English. After his arrival, he stayed with us, and later continued his studies at Salisbury College, pursuing a course in mechanical engineering. A couple of years later, Shahin started working with us in our business.

THE ROAD AHEAD

Running a nightclub and a restaurant was demanding. We worked long hours, often without a break, but were committed to making it a success. The team we built was crucial to our growth. Two Turkish brothers who had worked at *Caesars* had a unique flair for showmanship. One of them could perform a handstand while escorting customers to their tables, and the other could carry an unbelievable number of coffee cups. Their performances added a theatrical element to our service, drawing attention and making our establishment even more memorable.

We had no prior experience in running restaurants or nightclubs, but we were driven by our desire to succeed. Our lack of experience didn't stop us – it pushed us to learn quickly and adapt to the ever-changing demands of the business. And as we continued to grow, our hard work, creativity, and teamwork had paid off, making *Alcatraz* a well-known name on Bournemouth's nightlife and dining scene.

BUILDING THE ALCATRAZ EMPIRE

The concept of combining a restaurant and nightclub was bold for its time. With its prison-inspired space with metallic bars, dim lighting, and rock 'n' roll culture, *Alcatraz* stood out as a daring vision. Its aesthetics, blend of entertainment, food, and culture resonated with locals and the international students flocking to Bournemouth, with an eclectic mix of people, from businessmen to students, finding a place there. Our decision to not cater to everyone but to select members carefully added a sense of exclusivity that made *Alcatraz* even more desirable.

We began expanding rapidly, establishing an empire with a variety of concepts: restaurants, pubs and even a wholesale wine business. The businesses not only catered to the nightlife but expanded to offering food and beverage products in bulk, adding another income stream. The rise of *Alcatraz Wholesale* was a turning point – able to provide not just for our restaurants but also for others in the hospitality industry. It became a game-changer when Carlsberg moved its depot out of Bournemouth and we seized the opportunity to build our wine and spirits wholesale business, gaining traction with local bars and restaurants.

At Alcatraz Brasseries, we prided ourselves on delivering an authentic Italian dining experience. Our menu was meticulously crafted, and to ensure its authenticity, all our chefs were trained under the esteemed Franco Taruschio. Franco, an Italian chef awarded an OBE for his contributions to the culinary industry, ran the Walnut Tree Inn in Abergavenny, Wales with his wife Ann for thirty-seven years.

The ambience of our restaurants was designed to transport guests straight to Italy. With marble flooring, pristine white walls adorned with arches and beautiful bars showcasing a curated collection of imported fine Italian wines, the setting was both elegant and inviting. Artworks graced the walls, and tables were dressed in crisp white linens. Our staff, uniformed in ties and waistcoats paired with black trousers, added to the sophisticated atmosphere. In a couple of our establishments, charming waiters would escort ladies to their tables, dancing gracefully to the tunes of Italian music that played throughout the night. The ambience was magical. Many of our restaurants featured patio areas, allowing guests to enjoy their meals alfresco, embracing the Italian tradition of outdoor dining. To maintain a contemporary and smart aesthetic, we collaborated with a firm called Stone Design for much of our artwork. I took pride in importing all the restaurant furniture directly from Italy, ensuring authenticity in every detail. Our pubs, some of which were listed buildings with charming thatched roofs, were fitted out with a classic yet modern look and feel. They served traditional British food, sourced locally, and offered a selection of local beers alongside Italian, French, and new world wines. Our chefs were highly trained in British cuisine, and we introduced themed months where, in addition to the regular menu, we featured specialties from a particular country. For instance, during Italian month, guests could enjoy authentic Italian dishes, while Indian Month showcased a variety of Indian specialties. One of the most successful themes was French Month, which highlighted the beauty of French cuisine. Expanding our operations, I acquired a building that, after fitting it out, housed our head office on the mezzanine floor, with the ground floor operating as a warehouse. From there, we supplied wine, beer, soft drinks, and specialties like Kalamata olives and olive oil – sourced directly from Greece – to over 250 hotels, restaurants, and bars. We even supplied John Lewis at Brownsea Island in Poole, where they had a building for their partners to enjoy a holiday. Our fleet of trucks delivered goods all around the south-west, ensuring that our quality products reached a wide array of establishments. Our commitment to authenticity, quality, and exceptional service was the cornerstone of our success. By blending traditional elements with contemporary touches, we created spaces where guests could immerse themselves in rich culinary experiences, whether savouring Italian delicacies, enjoying British classics, or exploring international flavours during our themed months. Our dedication to sourcing the finest ingredients and collaborating with esteemed professionals like Franco ensured that every meal was memorable. The expansion into wholesale distribution further demonstrated our passion for sharing quality products with a broader audience, solidifying our reputation in the industry. Our restaurants expanded from Bournemouth and Poole to Winchester and Camberley, while our pubs extended into the New Forest.

Acquiring a hotel with a large function room was one of the biggest challenges of our operation. What we didn't know was that having a hotel means it is open twenty-four hours, with customers making demands any time of the day or night. Everything about running a hotel was difficult but we managed. We hosted many weddings, with brides needing lots of extra assistance. It all became part of what we excelled at providing.

In a relatively short time, we were running multiple sites, employing hundreds of people, and expanding our influence across the region. We were brand builders, always ahead of the curve with new concepts like the *Alcatraz Wine Bar*, which catered to business professionals by day and a younger, vibrant crowd by night. The late-night licence further cemented the place's relevance, and for more than twenty years it was a fixture in Bournemouth's nightlife.

The below were some of the designs and logos we used across various outlets and in the wholesale business.
They were created by Stone Studios.

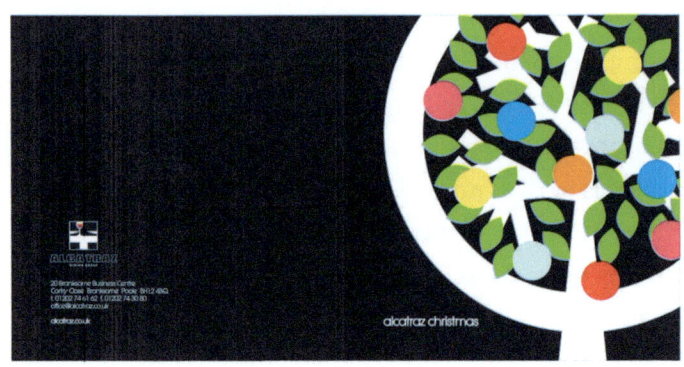

Shahab Hashtroudi

SIR JOHN BARLEYCORN
12TH CENTURY INN
NEW FOREST
OLD ROMSEY ROAD CADNAM HAMPSHIRE

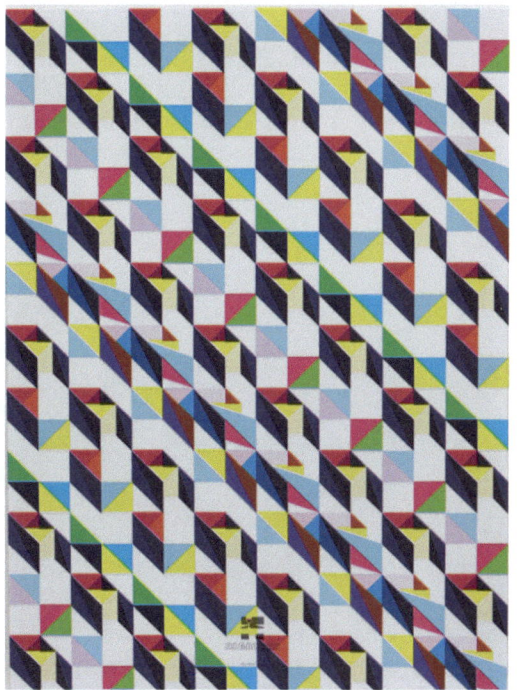

CLOSE FRIENDS AND SUPPORTERS

I met Angelo at a trade show in London while I was looking for a new wine supplier for our restaurants. We instantly clicked during that first meeting, and it marked the beginning of a long friendship and business relationship. Over the years, Angelo and I worked closely together, growing our businesses side by side.

We started by importing wine from Italy as part of a joint partnership. Later, when I opened my wholesale business, I became a wine distributor in south-west England. Vinum, Angelo's wholesale business started supplying Marks & Spencer with its well-known green label prosecco, created by Angelo.

Angelo and I met regularly, and on many occasions he invited me to visit Italy. During one of these trips, we travelled to Alba, Angelo's hometown, where I had the pleasure of meeting his parents. He introduced me to many fine restaurants in Italy, including those serving Michelin-starred meals. While I appreciated the culinary excellence, being a somewhat fussy eater I often found myself coming home hungry!

On another memorable trip to Sicily, Angelo introduced me to a local winemaker who owned a beautiful vineyard. The vineyard was managed by a remarkable woman who produced exquisite wine. These trips were filled with happy moments, strengthening both our business ties and friendship.

When I was incarcerated, Angelo made every effort to visit me, but sadly, he wasn't allowed. He was the first businessperson I met after my release. We reunited in London and shared a long, heartfelt lunch. Tragically, just a couple of years later when he was only fifty-nine years old, I received devastating news from his salesman, Sergio: Angelo had passed away that morning. At first, I couldn't believe it, but sadly, it was true. When I attended his funeral, it was one of the saddest days of my life. I had lost a great friend.

Jafar was another dear friend of mine, who I met when he was a customer at one of our restaurants. We developed a close friendship over the years. Jafar worked as a mortgage broker, and he played a pivotal role in helping me and my brother secure a mortgage for our first flat. I'll never forget the day he surprised us by ordering three beds, delivered straight to our garage, as a welcome-home present.

Years later, I received a call asking me to visit Jafar at a private hospital. When I arrived, I found him lying in bed. I asked what was wrong, and in response, he pulled back the bedsheet, revealing his testicles swollen to the size of melons. He had been diagnosed with prostate cancer and informed me that he didn't have much time left. Despite his own suffering, Jafar remained incredibly generous. During his hospital stay, he frequently ordered food from a local Indian restaurant for the doctors and nurses who cared for him. It was a testament to his kind-hearted nature.

After Jafar passed away, I attended his funeral. There, I met the owner of the Indian restaurant that had supplied the meals to the hospital. To my surprise, the owner revealed that Jafar had never paid for the food. It was a bittersweet reminder of Jafar's generous spirit and the moments we shared.

MYKONOS

During one of my sailing holidays to Mykonos, Greece, I met a man who rented motorbikes to tourists. He was doing well in his business, and one day, I saw him driving a brand-new Porsche Cayenne. As he pulled up to his shop, locals gathered around, cheering and clapping for his new car, which he had just picked up from the local Porsche dealership. Women even threw flowers at the car as part of the celebration.

When I asked about the occasion, I learned that in Mykonos, it's customary for friends and neighbours to celebrate someone's success. It was a heartwarming sight and a stark contrast to my experiences in England, where success often invites envy or criticism. Back home, if someone owns a nice car, it might get keyed, and if someone lives in a beautiful house, people might assume they are a drug dealer. This attitude is wrong. We should take a page from the people of Mykonos and learn to celebrate each other's achievements rather than resent them.

MEETING GABY

I met Gaby at *Alcatraz* club. She came in one night with a group of friends from Switzerland and was soon a regular while she was in Bournemouth learning English. We started going out with each other. Then she moved to Paris to complete her fashion design course. I would fly there to stay with her for few days, picking up ideas for the business from bars and restaurants in Paris. When she completed her course Gaby returned to Switzerland, visiting me in

Bournemouth frequently. We moved in together and then in the spring of 1989 we got married at Poole Registry Office, with her parents and my brothers and their girlfriends in attendance. Three days later, we all travelled to Zürich, where we had a church wedding service in a beautiful surrounding. It was magical. Sasha was born a year later and in 1995 we welcomed Nicole into the world. Both children were born in Zürich at a private hospital.

THE ALEX AND HUGO SAGA

That year, my brothers, their girlfriends, and I decided to spend Christmas and New Year's in the Canary Islands. It was meant to be a time of relaxation and fun, far away from the daily grind. We arrived at the resort, eager to make the most of our holiday. A few days later, Rody, Massoud's brother-in-law, joined us with his girlfriend.

One evening, while we were all gathered at a seaside restaurant for dinner, Rody dropped a bombshell. He casually mentioned something that would shake my world. 'Did you hear about Hugo and Alex?' he said.

Hugo, my manager at the Alcatraz Club, and Alex, the owner of Il Mondo – an Italian restaurant popular among foreign students – had gone behind my back. According to Rody, they had secretly partnered to open a nightclub just a few doors down from *Alcatraz*.

Il Mondo was strategically located in a neighbourhood where most of the foreign students lived. Every night, students would gather there, and from Alex's restaurant they would take taxis or buses to my club. It was a perfect synergy – or so I thought.

Now, Hugo and Alex were planning to poach my customers.

Their new club, set to open in a few weeks, was designed to steal the crowd I had worked so hard to cultivate. Worse still, Hugo had left his position at *Alcatraz* without so much as a word.

Naturally, I was furious.

Shahin, my brother, and his girlfriend had planned to leave the Canary Islands earlier than the rest of us. Seizing the opportunity, we decided to counter Hugo and Alex's move. Shahin purchased a minibus, branded it with the *Alcatraz Club* logo, and hired a driver. The idea was simple: offer students a free ride directly from Il Mondo to *Alcatraz*.

A few days later, I cut my holiday short and returned home with Gaby. I needed to confront Alex.

When I met him, I asked point-blank if the rumours were true. He admitted it. 'It's just business,' he said with a shrug, as though that excused the betrayal.

I didn't let their new club, Blah Blah, get the upper hand. Every night, the *Alcatraz* minibus parked outside Il Mondo, waiting to transport students – free of charge – to our club. The plan worked. *Alcatraz* was already an institution, with a reputation so strong that students arriving in the UK already knew it was the place to be.

Meanwhile, Blah Blah struggled to find its footing.

Alex, desperate to expand Il Mondo, leased the premises next door. He wanted to knock through the wall to create a larger space for his restaurant. But I wasn't done teaching him a lesson.

I approached my solicitor, David Ellis, and asked him to investigate who owned the freehold of Il Mondo's building. A few days later, David called with news. The freehold was owned by someone in Australia. Acting quickly, we reached out and made an offer.

Within weeks, I owned the freehold.

We sent Alex an official letter informing him of the change. From that moment on, he would have to pay rent to me. Predictably, he wasn't happy. When he asked for permission to knock through to the adjoining premises, I denied his request.

His anger didn't faze me. At the time, I was young, ambitious, and eager to prove a point.

Years later, Alex sold both his restaurant and nightclub. We met a couple of times after that, exchanged a few words, and even laughed about the past. But life has a way of catching up with all of us.

More recently, I went to Alex's funeral. Despite everything, I felt a pang of sadness. Our rivalry had been fierce, but it was part of what made those days unforgettable.

Looking back, I can't help but wish we had Facebook or Instagram back then. *Alcatraz* would have gone global, reaching millions. Still, those were some of the best years of my life – a time when ambition, loyalty, and betrayal shaped the stories we would one day tell.

THE BIGGEST SHOCK OF MY LIFE

Life threw another huge challenge my way in December 2001. Massoud's death from a sudden heart attack was a blow I could never have anticipated. It was undoubtedly the biggest shock of my life and it took a lot of time to process. The grief from losing a loved one is often overwhelming, and I found it hard to function. I retreated into myself and Gaby supported me during this painful period. Massoud's death left an irreplaceable hole in my life. Despite the support of my family, my mind remained elsewhere, and it affected both my work and personal lives.

Then, losing my mother in 2009, after a battle with Alzheimer's disease, compounded the emotional toll. I had chosen not to inform her of Massoud's passing, believing it would cause her unnecessary distress. This tough decision illustrates the deep care I had for her, and also how complex my personal journey had become.

AMBITION MEETS REALITY: FINANCIAL CRISIS

The rapid expansion came with its own set of challenges. The decision to grow quickly meant taking on significant amounts of debt. I relied on RBS for funding and the relationship seemed supportive at first. RBS encouraged my expansion plans, and I trusted its managers' guidance. However, as the global financial crisis of 2008 hit, everything changed and the recession became a harsh reality.

A knock on my door by two men from RBS was the start of a painful chapter. They informed me that my loan would be recalled within four weeks. I was blindsided. It was a difficult blow to absorb, especially when I had trusted the bank's advice to expand further. As RBS began calling in loans, I was forced to reconsider my entire business strategy. With the pressure mounting, I tried to salvage my empire. The decision to sell off sites and reduce the debt load was tough, but it was necessary.

The sale of sites wasn't enough, though, and the financial strain only deepened. I sought help from financial advisers and insolvency practitioners, but it soon became clear that the company was insolvent. This was a humbling experience, and facing liquidation meant not only the loss of my businesses but also of the life I had built. However, despite the financial turmoil, my resilience and willingness to adapt kept me afloat, allowing me to make the tough decisions required to survive.

Until the day the taxman came to call.

CHAPTER 14:
REFLECTIONS OF A FREE MAN

My time in prison was one of the most transformative periods of my life. I was incarcerated during a turbulent time and the experience shook me to my core. But, instead of succumbing to bitterness, I turned inward. Reading became a form of liberation and I began to see the world through a new lens of empathy, patience, and understanding.

Nelson Mandela's quotation about leaving behind bitterness resonated deeply with me and the hardship that I faced in prison allowed me to grow in ways I had not anticipated. Prison became a time of introspection, where I thought about my past mistakes and failures. During this time, I came to realise the importance of empathy, especially for those on the margins of society. I learned about addiction, poverty, and abuse. These issues had been distant from my personal experience but now became a central part of my understanding of the world.

PERSONAL LESSONS LEARNED

As I reflect on my life, key lessons emerge loud and clear:

■ Focus on Family
Always working tirelessly, often at the expense of family time, is something that I now regret. While I poured energy into growing my businesses and providing for our employees, my family life became strained. My divorce and my separation from my son, Sasha, are reminders that success should never come at the cost of personal relationships.

■ Build a Proper Foundation
While I built a business empire for others, sometimes I didn't construct enough of a foundation for myself. Taking risks, being passionate about what I do and never being afraid to challenge the status quo were principles that drove my success. However, they also carried consequences. I learned the hard way that balance, both in work and in personal life, is the true key to happiness and fulfilment.

■ Define Your Happiness
Looking back, I see the full picture. The journey that began with a small investment in a coffee shop turned into a thriving business empire, only to end in financial ruin. But what's most important is the wisdom I have gained along the way. The transformation in how I view success – no longer about accumulating wealth or expanding endlessly, but now about finding peace, purpose, and balance – marks my true growth.

■ Live Authentically

As I have learned, life is unpredictable. It is not the highs and lows that define you but the lessons that you take from them. I have embraced this philosophy and, despite many struggles, I have emerged stronger.

MY PERSONAL RELATIONSHIPS

Father and Mother are etched into my heart. I will never forget the day Father suddenly passed away. In separation from him, I felt myself cast into emptiness as relentless tears washed away all of my patience. I did not know where to turn once my guide had left me alone in this world of conflict and confusion. How could I carry on without his love, his smile and his wisdom?

Now that I realise his presence was always with me in my heart and it will remain there, along with the love I have developed for others, showing them the love that my father and mother always showed to me.

Hedi and Shahin both live in the Bournemouth area and we see each other regularly. Stavy and I started out as businesspeople exchanging ideas and telling each other our problems. Our friendship grew into love.

I have always loved Gaby and still do, even now we are divorced. Strangely, we have become closer and we are very good friends. We're always in contact with each other and I wish her all the very best in her life. Nicole is happy living in Australia. She has a great job as a marketing executive in a furniture company. She loves the life in Australia, the weather and the outdoor life. She has many friends and some very close friends who travelled to Australia from UK are all still living together in Sydney. I love her dearly and would love to visit and spend some time with her.

Sasha, now married with Hannah with a four-year-old son called Bodhi, lives in a beautiful house in Christchurch, Dorset and works as a solicitor in Southampton. I love him and miss him dearly.

Letters show the deep relationship we still share.

Dear Gaby,
Thank you for yesterday
I hope you're doing well. I've been thinking a lot about everything you went through when I went to prison, and I feel I need to say this to you.

When I got prosecuted and everything fell apart, you had to handle so much on your own. You managed to sell properties, and dealt with the HMRC situation – all while trying to keep things stable for Sasha and Nicole. I know it wasn't easy, especially with how public and media and everything was.

On top of all that, you were there for Sasha and Nicole helping them to get on with their life during such a difficult time. I can only imagine how hard it was for them, and for you, to carry the weight of it all.

Gaby, I want you to know that I see how much you went through, and I don't take it lightly. I'm deeply grateful for everything you did to keep things together when I couldn't.

Even though we're no longer married, I value the friendship we have and the amazing mother you've been to Sasha and Nicole. Thank you for everything – you truly did more than anyone could have asked.

Take care. Lots of love as always Shab

Thank you Shahab ❤ *this means a lot to me!*

Yes, it wasn't easy but I did it, don't know how but it's done. Probably been scr...ed a few times over by some people but it's the past!

I appreciate our friendship very much, we've had a loving past, not just tears but fun and love and I like to think back to the good times!

Hope the sun will shine again for all of us! Lots of love
Gaby

ADVICE FOR BUSINESSES IN HARD FINANCIAL TIMES

- Focus on the right things.
- Solve problems that your customers care about.
- Think long-term, while making bold moves.
- Simplify, prioritise, execute.
- Put survival over your ego.
- Invest in good advice.

The biggest mistake I ever made was going through legal aid to hire defence lawyers for our criminal case. The total bill for all three brothers came to £800,000. Including the accountant and the directors defence team, the total came to more than £1m and we all got a poor and unprofessional defence. In hindsight, I should have hired a private firm to defend all of us and choose a better legal team. I am very sure that the outcome would have been different if I had.

Many years ago, I learned a good lesson by instructing a very good barrister to act for me to get an extension in the operating licence of our nightclub. He had written several books on licensing law and on the morning of the magistrate's hearing, he put one of his books upright with his picture printed on the cover facing the magistrates and clerk of justice. He made an application to the magistrates, explaining where they stood on the matter in law and told them he had written many articles on licensing in his books. He even showed the book to the magistrates later when answering their questions. The result was that an extension in nightclub licensing hours was granted for the first time in the Bournemouth area. This was the best money I ever spent on legal representation and shows that using a good, capable, honest barrister can win your case.

My advice is to everyone who has a court hearing get the best defence team you can afford, even if you have to re-mortgage your house.

LESSONS FOR LAWYERS

I still feel stung and harshly treated by a conviction that I still maintain was wrong and unjust, so I make no apologies for finding as many lessons for lawyers as for myself.

■ Prepare Properly and Communicate Well
The lawyers acting for our group barely reviewed their case files, skimmed through evidence, and did not bother to meet with their clients to understand their story. When they did meet, it often felt rushed and dismissive and they did not take notes. In court, they stumbled through their statements, unprepared and unfamiliar with key details. Our lawyers were also hard to reach, rarely returning phone calls or emails from clients. When they did communicate,

they were often condescending or indifferent, making us feel like a burden and in the dark about our cases.

■ Act in Clients' Best Interests and Be Professional in and out of the Courtroom

Our lawyers didn't seem to care about achieving an outcome in our best interest of their clients. I am sure that, halfway through the hearing, a deal was made with the prosecution barrister without me being informed or asked for consent. My barrister also told me that he wanted to be careful in court as he wanted the jury to like him. I was not interested in the jury falling in love with him. I just wanted him to be professional and have the courage to tell the judge that he was making a mistake.

On one occasion when we were in court, I could see one of the defence barristers looking online at a restaurant menu for The Ivy while my brother was giving evidence. Judge Henry had reminded all the barristers to be in court early the next morning, so it was clear that the lawyer was minded to stay the night and thinking about where to eat, instead of him concentrating on the case. It was also lame of my barrister to use a light dusting of snow as an excuse for not attending my sentencing. Everybody else managed to travel.

■ Know Your Law and Strategy and Be Organised

Our lawyers struggled with basic legal concepts and could not effectively cross-examine witnesses or respond to objections. They didn't think strategically and failed to anticipate the prosecution's approach, put together a coherent defence or properly consider bringing in relevant experts or witnesses. None of our barristers understood catering operations and accounts.

■ Do What Is Right and Resist Pressure from Those with Power
When I asked the firm of lawyers our businesses had been using for
thirty years to help us to find a criminal lawyer, they were put under
pressure not to act for us by HMRC. The founder of our auditors
and accountants, who we had worked with for more than thirty-five
years, was also pressured to not assist us and did not turn up to give
evidence, though a younger accountant from that firm who I had
never dealt with did give evidence against us.

In addition, one of my in-house accountants, who I helped to
complete his training and become chartered, left us two years before
the investigation. He was called as a witness and twice changed his
evidence under oath, telling me had been pressured to do so by
HMRC. An accountant who worked for us for two years similarly
changed her plea twice. Tracy, who was convicted and given a two-
year suspended sentence, was pressured to change her statement,
but refused to do so. Garth, another in-house accountant, also
would not change his statement.

I will never forget their honesty and I will forever be grateful for
their courage

LESSONS FOR JUDGES

■ Be truly impartial
Avoid giving any indication of personal opinions about the guilt
or innocence of defendants. The role of a judge is to interpret and
apply the law, not to make determinations on guilt. If evidence is

objectionable or a witness's testimony is irrelevant, judges may step in to make rulings, but they must explain these rulings impartially, focusing on legal grounds without adding subjective commentary. In instances where judges need to intervene due to inappropriate behaviour by one party, they should do so with professionalism, applying the same standard to both sides.

■ Give Juries Clear and Neutral Instructions
When providing instructions to the jury on how to interpret the law and approach deliberations, they should be clear, complete, and neutral. Judges instructing juries at the end of trials should clarify that jurors alone are responsible for deciding on the facts and determining guilt or innocence based on the evidence and that their decision must be made without any influence from anyone else, including the judge. Judges must be held to a high standard of neutrality to ensure the integrity of the justice system.

■ Treat Both Sides Equally
Judges should allow both the prosecution and defence to make their arguments without showing favouritism, treat lawyers and witnesses for both sides with equal respect, and allow each time to fully present evidence and testimony. This was not the case with Judge Henry, who was clearly biased towards the prosecution.

■ Keep Personal Reactions Under Control
Even subtle body language or tone of voice can influence a jury's perception. Good judges remain aware of their reactions and avoid showing signs of frustration, scepticism, or approval when attorneys

or witnesses are speaking or giving evidence. On a number of occasions in our case, Judge Henry did not have control over his body language or tone of his voice, which influenced the jury's perception. I did complain a number of times to my legal team. Nothing was done about it.

THE FUTURE

Nearly four decades have passed since my business journey started by opening a coffee shop and trying to build an empire.

My businesses became successful after tweaking and hard work. I got married and had two beautiful children who have now both graduated from university and are succeeding in their lives and careers. I have always tried to provide for my family, my employees, and others through some charity work.

Companies survive only by delivering what customer truly care about. Mastering that one essential need is the foundation. Everything else is secondary. I was supported in meeting customers' needs by many people who really cared and helped me to grow the business. I was lucky to have my brothers to help and support all the people who helped us run the outlets.

I remained on release from prison under licence until February 1, 2025. Two days later, I left Britain for a long holiday in Thailand and Vietnam with Stavy. I now do some consultancy work for a hotel group and individual restaurateurs and a wholesale business, and try to help businesses, especially the ones that they are having trouble to keep their head above water.

I enjoy helping others. I would also like to travel the world and learn more about other countries and cultures. This shooting star still has a great deal of momentum.

ACKNOWLEDGEMENTS

The people who really stood by us with the business were Garth Mathews, Tracy Shaw, our executive chefs Jed King and Radwan Wolly and our in-house IT engineer Mark Bajaj.

Externally, I am also grateful to David Ellis, Desmond Leyden, our solicitor Rob Kelly and Brian Hutchinson, our auditor. In prison, Maria Arpa trained me in the DRM team, while Lee Middleton and Roger were the best of the officers, as well as being my boss in DRM and the textile works.

During my prison journey, I very much appreciated the full support of close friends who wrote to me regularly and were my lifeline to the outside world.

Stavy Antoniou, Gaby, Sasha and Nicole Hashtroudi, Mohsen Nami, Siamak Ghaisary and Rob Kelly, I want to thank you all. I was so grateful for every visit, letter, or email I received from you.

When a disaster occurs in your life, you really realise who your real friends are. True friends stay with you forever.